CREATION AND EVOLUTION

CREATION
and
EVOLUTION

A Conference with Pope

BENEDICT XVI

in Castel Gandolfo

Published on behalf of
the former postgraduate students of Pope Benedict XVI
by Stephan Otto Horn, S.D.S., and Siegfried Wiedenhofer

Foreword by Christoph Cardinal Schönborn

Translated by Michael J. Miller

IGNATIUS PRESS   SAN FRANCISCO

Original German edition:
Schöpfung und Evolution
Eine Tagung mit Papst Benedikt XVI. in Castel Gandolfo
© 2007 by Libreria Editrice Vaticana, Rome
© 2007 by Sankt Ulrich Verlag GmbH, Augsburg

Cover art by
Michelangelo Buonarroti (1475–1564)
The Sistine Chapel ceiling frescos after restoration
The Creation of the Sun, Moon and Planets
The Sistine Chapel, Vatican Palace, Vatican State

Photo Credit: Erich Lessing / Art Resource, N.Y.

Cover by John Herreid, based on the German original

ISBN 978-1-58617-234-3
Library of Congress Control Number 2007938139
Printed in the United States of America ∞

CONTENTS

FOREWORD

We are not some casual and meaningless product of evolution. Each of us is the result of a thought of God. Each of us is willed, each of us is loved, each of us is necessary.

> —Sermon of Pope Benedict XVI at the Mass for the inauguration of his pontificate

In 1985 a symposium took place in Rome on the topic of "Evolutionism and Christianity". It was organized by Professor Robert Spaemann and his professorial chair in the philosophy faculty in Munich. It was hosted by the Holy See's Congregation for the Doctrine of the Faith under the direction of its prefect at that time, Cardinal Joseph Ratzinger. What the current Holy Father wrote then in his "Preface" to the published proceedings of this symposium[1] can very well serve as an introduction to the proceedings of the colloquium that his circle of former students[2] had the privilege of holding, at his invitation, from September 1–3, 2006, in Castel Gandolfo.

There was no lack of media interest in this meeting of the *Schülerkreis*. The debate about creation and evolution,

---

[1] R. Spaemann, R. Löw, and P. Koslowski, eds., *Evolutionismus und Christentum* (Weinheim, 1986), vii–ix.

[2] The *Schülerkreis* is the circle of former doctoral and postdoctoral candidates that has met almost annually with their *Doktorvater* [dissertation advisor] for the past twenty-five years or so.

7

about faith and science, about design or chance in the process by which our world came to be has made big waves in recent months. My article in the July 7, 2005, issue of *The New York Times* was something of a catalyst in this phenomenon. Of course, the debate has been going on for so long that it is part of the intellectual atmosphere. It has been revived again and again by many factors, and it is far from being over. And it is urgently needed. In numerous commentaries, Pope Benedict XVI has tried to explain why this is so.

Many apprehensions have been voiced in recent months, as though the Church might revise her position with regard to belief in the creation and the teaching of evolution. But what exactly is the Church's view about this question? No one is better qualified to say than the longtime Prefect of the Congregation for the Doctrine of the Faith, the eminent theologian and teacher Pope Benedict XVI. In the following pages, therefore, some of his statements on this subject should be cited at greater length. Let us begin with a rather long quotation from the preface to the collection of papers from the 1986 symposium:

> The debate between faith and the teaching of evolution, which was conducted with some vehemence in the nineteenth and early twentieth centuries, seemed to have reached a somewhat peaceful resolution by the middle of this century. The encyclical *Humani generis*, dated August 12, 1950, had left the question of the origin of individual living species to the competence of research in the natural sciences and had merely stated the anthropological proviso that man cannot be explained solely in terms of biological factors; as a living being endowed with a soul, each one is a new beginning that cannot be derived from biological precursors but

points to the Creator. This truce, of course, did not entirely smooth over the argument about man: soon afterward even theologians no longer knew what to do with the concept of "soul" and its direct creation by God. The classical anthropological model, in which the indispensability of faith was formulated, could not be easily reconciled with the completely different intellectual point of departure of evolutionary theory and its comprehensive explanatory claim, which was unwilling to stop short of man.

At about the same time a new vision became popular, in which Teilhard de Chardin attempted to unite the totality of the natural sciences and of their way of thinking with the totality of the theological view of man. No doubt many and various fruitful ideas came out of Teilhard's intuitions, which enriched the philosophical and theological dialogue with the natural sciences. They could not provide a definitive answer, because his foundations in the natural sciences were limited essentially to the fields of anatomy and morphology (excluding the genetic processes), and his development of philosophical and theological concepts remained unsatisfactory as well.

Today a new stage of the debate has been reached, inasmuch as "evolution" has been exalted above and beyond its scientific content and made into an intellectual model that claims to explain the whole of reality and thus has become a sort of "first philosophy". Whereas the Middle Ages had attempted a "derivation of all science from theology" (Bonaventure), we can speak here about a derivation of all reality from "evolution", which believes that it can also account for knowledge, ethics, and religion in terms of the general scheme of evolution. The fact that this philosophy presents itself as an apparently neat explanation of the findings of the natural sciences and frankly identifies itself with that knowledge gives it an almost incontestable plausibility, which in the midst of the general crisis in philosophical thought is all the more effective.

9

If we carefully examine this development in the evolution question, then it is obvious that we are faced here with a completely new situation in the dialogue, which cannot be measured by the parameters of the nineteenth-century dispute between natural science and theology. At that time too, admittedly, there were philosophical extrapolations from scientific knowledge that wrongly claimed the certainty of the latter as a basis for unproven conceptual models. But today's form of evolutionary philosophy—which seems, so to speak, to look only on the whole of scientific knowledge and thus at the same time intends to offer an insight into the fabric of being, down to its ultimate foundations and out to its most specific developments—is nevertheless something new. Here the borders and transitions between natural science and philosophy are, on the one hand, quite often very difficult to define but, on the other hand, extremely consequential, because the coherence of the whole excludes any other explanatory principle. The derivation of all reality from matter thus attains a totality that in the nineteenth century was still scarcely imaginable.

Whereas faith today no longer has any difficulty in allowing the scientific hypothesis of evolution to develop in peace according to its own methods, the absolute claim of the philosophical explanatory model "evolution" is an all the more radical challenge to faith and theology. It is obvious that reinterpretations, "retoolings", are often far more dangerous than flat denials. So it is even more important to find the correct level of discourse on this subject. In no case should the appearance of a new dispute between natural science and faith be created, because in fact that is not at all what this dialogue is about. The real level of discourse is that of philosophical thought: when natural science becomes a philosophy, it is up to philosophy to grapple with it. Only in that way is the contentious issue framed correctly; only then does it remain clear what we are dealing with: a rational, philosophical debate that aims at the objectivity of rational knowledge, and not a protest of faith against reason.

It was not first in his famous Regensburg Address that the Holy Father emphasized the importance of reason in mediating between natural science and faith. Almost forty years ago Professor Ratzinger took the same basic position on this issue as we find impressively taken in 1986 in the passage just cited. In a series of radio talks broadcast by the *Süddeutscher Rundfunk* in 1968, the theologian, who at that time was teaching in Tübingen, expressed at great length his opinion on the subject of "belief in creation and the theory of evolution". We reprint here a major portion of this talk:[3]

In order to move forward, we must examine more closely both the creation account and also the idea of evolution; both of these things, unfortunately, are possible here only in outline form. Let us ask first, then, starting with the latter topic: How does one actually understand the world when it is viewed in evolutionary terms? An essential component, of course, is the notion that being and time enter into a fixed relation: being *is* time; it does not merely *have* time. Only in becoming does it exist and unfold into itself. Accordingly, being is understood dynamically, as being-in-movement, and it is understood as something directed: it does not always revolve around the same state of affairs but rather advances. Admittedly, there is a debate over whether the concept of progress can be applied to the evolutionary chain, especially since there is no neutral standard available that would allow us to say specifically what should be

[3] "Schöpfungsglaube und Evolutionstheorie", in H.J. Schulz, ed., *Wer ist das eigentlich—Gott?* (Munich, 1969), 232–45. Also in *Dogma und Verkündigung*, 4th ed. (Donauwörth, 2005), 152–56.

regarded as better or less good and consequently when we could seriously speak of an advance.

Nevertheless, the special relation that man assumes with respect to all the rest of reality entitles him to regard himself as the point of reference, at least for the question about himself: insofar as he is at issue, he is no doubt justified in doing so. And when he measures in this way, the direction of evolution and its progressive character are ultimately indisputable, even if one takes into account the fact that there are dead ends in evolution and that its path by no means runs in a straight line. Detours, too, are a path, and by way of detours, too, one arrives at the goal, as evolution itself demonstrates. Of course the question remains open whether being, understood in such a way as a path—that is, evolution as a whole—has a meaning, and it cannot be decided within the theory of evolution itself; for that theory this is a methodologically foreign question, although of course for a live human being it is the fundamental question of the whole thing. Science rightly acknowledges its limits in this regard and declares that this question, which is indispensable for man, cannot be answered within science, but only within the framework of a "faith system". We need not be concerned here with the opinion of many people that the Christian "faith system" is unsuited to answering this question and that a new one must be found, because they thereby make a statement within their own faith decision and outside the parameters of their science.

With that, however, we are now in a position to say precisely what the belief in creation means with regard to the evolutionary understanding of the world. Confronted with the fundamental question, which cannot be answered by evolutionary theory itself, of whether meaninglessness or meaning [Sinn] prevails, this belief expresses the conviction that the world as a whole, as the Bible says, comes from the Logos, that is, from creative mind [Sinn] and represents the temporal form of its self-actuation. From the perspective of our understanding of the world, creation is not a distant beginning or a beginning divided up into several stages, but rather it concerns being as something temporal and becoming: temporal being as a whole is encompassed by the one creative act of God, which, in its division, gives it its unity, in which at the same time its meaning consists, a meaning that is unfathomable to us because we do not see the whole but are ourselves only parts of it. Belief in creation does not tell us what the meaning of the world is but only that there is one: the whole back and forth of being-in-becoming is the free and therefore inherently risky actuation of the primordial creative thought from which it has its being. And so today, perhaps, we can understand better what the Christian dogma of creation was always saying but could hardly bring to bear because of the influence of the model from antiquity: creation should be thought of, not according to the model of the craftsman who makes all sorts of objects, but rather in the manner in which thought is creative. And at the same time it becomes evident that being-in-movement as a whole (and not just the beginning) is creation and that likewise the whole (and not merely what comes later) is, properly speaking, reality and its proper movement. To summarize all this, we can say: To believe in creation means to understand, in faith, the world of becoming revealed by science as a meaningful world that comes from a creative mind.

But this already clearly delineates also the answer to the question about the creation of man, because now the foundational decision about the place of spirit and meaning in the world has been made: the recognition of the world of becoming as the self-actuation of a creative thought includes also its derivation from the creativity of the spirit, from the *Creator Spiritus*. In the writings of Teilhard de Chardin we find the following ingenious comment on this question:

"What distinguishes a materialist from a spiritualist is no longer, by any means (as in philosophy, which establishes fixed concepts) the fact that he admits a transition between the physical infrastructure and the psychic superstructure of things, but *only* the fact that he incorrectly sets the *definitive* point of equilibrium in the cosmic movement on the side of the infrastructure, that is, on the side of disintegration." Certainly one can debate the details in this formulation; yet the decisive point seems to me to be grasped quite accurately: the alternative: materialism or a spiritually defined world view, chance or meaning, is presented to us today in the form of the question of whether one regards spirit and life in its ascending forms as an incidental mold on the surface of the material world (that is, of the category of existing things that do not understand themselves), or whether one regards spirit as the goal of the process and, conversely, matter as the prehistory of the spirit. If one chooses the second alternative, it is clear that spirit is not a random product of material developments, but rather that matter signifies a moment in the history of spirit. This, however, is just another way of saying that spirit is created and not the mere product of development, even though it comes to light by way of development.

With that we have reached the point at which we can answer the question of how in fact the theological statement about the special creation of man can coexist with an evolutionary world view or what form it must assume within an evolutionary world view. To discuss this in detail would naturally go beyond the parameters of this essay; a few notes must suffice. We should recall first that, with respect to the creation of man, too, "creation" does not designate a remote beginning but rather has each of us in view along with Adam: every human being *is* directly in relation to God. The faith declares no more about the first man than it does about each one of us, and, conversely, it declares no less about us than it does about the first man.

Every human being is more than the product of inherited traits and environment; no one results exclusively from calculable this-worldly factors; the mystery of creation looms over every one of us. This would then lead to the insight that spirit does not enter the picture as something foreign, as a second substance in addition to matter; the appearance of spirit, according to the previous discussion, means rather that an advancing movement arrives at the goal that has been set for it. Finally it would have to be noted that, of all things, the creation of spirit is least of all to be imagined as an artisan activity of God, who suddenly began tinkering with the world.

If creation means dependence of being, then special creation is nothing other than special dependence of being. The statement that man is created in a more specific, more direct way by God than other things in nature, when expressed somewhat less metaphorically, means simply this: that man is willed by God in a specific way, not merely as a being that "is there", but as a being that knows him; not only as a construct that he thought up, but as an existence that can think about him in return. We call the fact that man is specifically willed and known by God his special creation.

From this vantage point, one can immediately make a diagnosis about the form of anthropogenesis: The clay became man at that moment in which a being for the first time was capable of forming, however dimly, the thought "God". The first Thou that—however stammeringly—was said by human lips to God marks the moment in which spirit arose in the world. Here the Rubicon of anthropogenesis was crossed. For it is not the use of weapons or fire, not new methods of cruelty or of useful activity, that constitute man, but rather his ability to be immediately in relation to God. This holds fast to the doctrine of the special creation of man; herein lies the center of belief in creation in the first place. Herein also lies the reason why the moment of anthropogenesis cannot possibly be determined by paleontology: anthropogenesis is the rise of the spirit, which cannot be excavated with a shovel. The theory of evolution does not invalidate the faith, nor does it corroborate it. But it does challenge the faith to understand itself more profoundly and thus to help man to understand himself and to become increasingly what he is: the being who is supposed to say Thou to God in eternity.

As a theologian, the Holy Father pointed out early on the shortage of teaching about creation in broad sectors of contemporary theology and has repeatedly warned about the consequences of this "practical abandonment of the doctrine of creation".[4] As Archbishop of Munich, Cardinal Ratzinger therefore gave a prominent place to the theme of creation in his preaching. The four Lenten sermons that he preached in early 1981 attest to this. Soon afterward Pope John Paul II called him to Rome and appointed him to the Curia. In 1985 he wrote, "In the years following, from the perspective of my new work, the critical state of the creation issue in present-day proclamation has become still more evident." [5]

The famous speech on the state of catechesis that he gave in the cathedrals of Lyons and Paris[6] vigorously emphasized the necessity of a renewal in catechesis about creation as the foundation for any proclamation of salvation. In 1985

[4] Joseph Cardinal Ratzinger, *In the Beginning: A Catholic Understanding of the Story of Creation and the Fall*, trans. Boniface Ramsey, O.P. (Grand Rapids, Mich.: Eerdmans, 1995), x. [Original German edition: *Im Anfang schuf Gott: Vier Münchener Fastenpredigten über Schöpfung und Fall* (Munich, 1986), 9].

[5] Ibid., ix–x.

[6] Joseph Cardinal Ratzinger, "Handing on the Faith and the Sources of the Faith", in *Handing on the Faith in an Age of Disbelief*, trans. Michael J. Miller (San Francisco: Ignatius Press, 2006), 13–40.

the Fathers of the Extraordinary Session of the Synod of Bishops requested that Pope John Paul II commission the production of a catechism of the Second Vatican Council. In 1986 the Pope appointed his trusted assistant, Cardinal Ratzinger, the head of the commission responsible for composing the desired catechism.

It is no wonder, therefore, that the Catholic doctrine concerning creation occupies considerable space in the new *Catechism of the Catholic Church* (nos. 279–384). Many have criticized the *Catechism* for not explicitly stating an opinion on the subject of evolution. Even though the word itself does not appear, the matter is clearly addressed (cf. nos. 283–85). It is not the purpose of the *Catechism* to lead a discussion about belief in creation and evolutionary teaching. Other forums are more appropriate for that.

In a very prominent forum for intellectual discussion, at the Sorbonne in Paris, Cardinal Ratzinger gave a talk on November 27, 1999, which to my knowledge is the most detailed opinion about our theme that he has penned. Therefore it should be cited here also *in extenso*:[7]

> The separation of physics from metaphysics achieved by Christian thinking is being steadily canceled. Everything is to become "physics" again. The theory of evolution has increasingly emerged as the way to make metaphysics disappear, to make "the hypothesis of God" (Laplace) superfluous, and to formulate a strictly "scientific" explanation of the world. A comprehensive theory of evolution, intended to explain the whole of reality, has become a kind of "first philosophy", which represents, as it were, the true foundation for

[7] Reprinted in Joseph Cardinal Ratzinger, *Truth and Tolerance: Christian Belief and World Religions*, trans. Henry Taylor (San Francisco: Ignatius Press, 2004), 178–83 [translation slightly amended].

an enlightened understanding of the world. Any attempt to involve any basic elements other than those worked out within the terms of such a "positive" theory, any attempt at "metaphysics", necessarily appears as a regression from enlightenment, as abandoning the universal claims of science. Thus the Christian idea of God is necessarily regarded as unscientific. There is no longer any *theologia physica* (θελογία φυσική) that corresponds to it: in this view, the doctrine of evolution is the only *theologia naturalis*, and that knows of no God, either a creator in the Christian (or Jewish or Islamic) sense or a world-soul or moving spirit in the Stoic sense. One could, at any rate, regard this whole world as mere appearance and nothingness as the true reality and, thus, justify some forms of mystical religion, which are at least not in direct competition with enlightenment.

Has the last word been spoken? Have Christianity and reason permanently parted company? There is at any rate no getting around the dispute about the extent of the claims of the doctrine of evolution as a fundamental philosophy and about the exclusive validity of the positive method as the sole indicator of systematic knowledge and of rationality. This dispute has therefore to be approached objectively and with a willingness to listen, by both sides—something that has hitherto been undertaken only to a limited extent. No one will be able to cast serious doubt upon the scientific evidence for micro-evolutionary processes. R. Junker and S. Scherer, in their "critical reader" on evolution, have this to say: "Many examples of such developmental steps [micro-evolutionary processes] are known to us from natural processes of variation and development. The research done on them by evolutionary biologists produced significant knowledge of the adaptive capacity of living systems, which seems ingenious." They tell us, accordingly, that one would therefore be quite justified in describing origins research as the reigning monarch among biological disciplines.

It is not toward that point, therefore, that a believer will direct the questions that he puts to modern rationality but rather toward the development of evolutionary theory into a generalized *philosophia universalis*, which claims to constitute a universal explanation of reality and is unwilling to allow the continuing existence of any other level of thinking. Within the teaching about evolution itself, the problem emerges at the point of transition from micro- to macroevolution, on which point Szathmáry and Maynard Smith, both convinced supporters of an all-embracing theory of evolution, nonetheless declare that: "There is no theoretical basis for believing that evolutionary lines become more complex with time; and there is also no empirical evidence that this happens."

The question that has now to be put certainly delves deeper: it is whether the theory of evolution can be presented as a universal theory concerning all reality, beyond which further questions about the origin and the nature of things are no longer admissible and indeed no longer necessary, or whether such ultimate questions do not after all go beyond the realm of what can be entirely the object of research and knowledge by natural science. I should like to put the question in still more concrete form. Has everything been said with the kind of answer that we find thus formulated by Popper: "Life as we know it consists of physical 'bodies' (more precisely, structures) which are problem solving. This the various species have 'learned' by natural selection, that is to say, by the method of reproduction plus variation, which itself has been learned by the same method. This regress is not necessarily infinite..."? I do not think so. In the end this concerns a choice that can no longer be made on purely scientific grounds or basically on philosophical grounds. The question is whether reason, or rationality, stands at the beginning of all things and upon their foundation or not.

The question is whether reality originated on the basis of chance and necessity (or, as Popper says, in agreement with Butler, on the basis of luck and cunning) and, thus, from what is irrational; that is, whether reason, being a chance by-product of irrationality and floating in an ocean of irrationality, is ultimately just as meaningless; or whether the principle that represents the fundamental conviction of Christian faith and of its philosophy remains true: "In principio erat Verbum"—at the beginning of all things stands the creative power of reason. Now as then, Christian faith represents the choice in favor of the priority of reason and of rationality. This ultimate question, as we have already said, can no longer be decided by arguments from natural science, and even philosophical thought reaches its limits here. In that sense, there is no ultimate demonstration that the basic choice involved in Christianity is correct. Yet, can reason really renounce its claim to the priority of what is rational over the irrational, the claim that the Logos is at the ultimate origin of things, without abolishing itself? The explanatory model presented by Popper, which reappears in different variations in the various accounts of the "basic philosophy", shows that reason cannot do other than to think of irrationality according to its own standards, that is, those of reason (solving problems, learning methods!), so that it implicitly reintroduces nonetheless the primacy of reason, which has just been denied. Even today, by virtue of its choosing to assert the primacy of reason, Christianity remains "enlightened", and I think that any enlightenment that cancels this choice must, contrary to all appearances, mean, not an evolution, but an involution, a shrinking, of enlightenment.

We saw before that in the way early Christianity saw things, the concepts of nature, man, God, ethics, and religion were indissolubly linked together and that this very interlinking contributed to make Christianity appear the obvious choice in the crisis concerning the gods and in the crisis concerning the enlightenment of the ancient world. The orientation of religion toward a rational view of reality as a whole, ethics as a part of this vision, and its concrete application under the primacy of love became closely associated. The primacy of the Logos and the primacy of love proved to be identical. The Logos was seen to be, not merely a mathematical reason at the basis of all things, but a creative love taken to the point of becoming sympathy, suffering with the creature. The cosmic aspect of religion, which reverences the Creator in the power of being, and its existential aspect, the question of redemption, merged together and became one.

Every explanation of reality that cannot at the same time provide a meaningful and comprehensible basis for ethics necessarily remains inadequate. Now the theory of evolution, in the cases where people have tried to extend it to a *philosophia universalis*, has in fact been used for an attempt at a new ethos based on evolution. Yet this evolutionary ethic that inevitably takes as its key concept the model of selectivity, that is, the struggle for survival, the victory of the fittest, successful adaptation, has little comfort to offer. Even when people try to make it more attractive in various ways, it ultimately remains a cruel ethic. Here, the attempt to distill rationality out of what is in itself irrational quite visibly fails. All this is of very little use for an ethic of universal peace, of practical love of one's neighbor, and of the necessary overcoming of oneself, which is what we need.

The attempt, in this crisis for mankind, to give back an obvious meaning and significance to the concept of Christianity as the *religio vera* must, so to speak, be based in equal measure upon orthopraxy and orthodoxy. At the most profound level its content will necessarily consist—in the final analysis, just as it did then—in love and reason coming together as the two pillars of reality: the true reason is love, and love is the true reason. They are in their unity the true basis and the goal of all reality.

In his interview with Peter Seewald, Cardinal Ratzinger once again very briefly summarizes what is at issue also in the discussion recorded in this volume: "The Christian picture of the world is this, that the world in its details is the product of a long process of evolution but that at the most profound level it comes from the *Logos*. Thus it carries rationality within itself." [8]

Investigating this Logos, studying and fathoming the "intelligent design that is the cosmos", [9] is possible only because reality is "reasonable" and hence can be studied by our reason. But more on that in the proceedings of the colloquium itself.

Now, however, we still have to express our thanks. First and foremost to the Holy Father himself. Since his election he has generously invited the *Schülerkreis* to Castel Gandolfo twice already and set aside much time to converse with his former students. Whereas the first day of our meeting last year [2006] was devoted to the preparatory discussion within the *Schülerkreis*, it was our great joy that the Holy Father personally participated during the entire second day, on September 2. His comments on the individual presentations are recorded in the transcription of the discussion.

For this transcription we thank Mrs. Jutta Lang, and for the edited version of the contributions to the discussion—which were approved by all the participants—we are grate-

[8] *God and the World*, trans. Henry Taylor (San Francisco: Ignatius Press, 2002), 139.

[9] "Progetto intelligente che è il cosmo", General Audience of November 9, 2005.

ful to Professor Siegfried Wiedenhofer and his wife. We owe a debt of thanks to the publishing house Sankt Ulrich Verlag and its director, Dr. Dirk Hermann Voss, and his assistant, Dr. Peter Paul Bornhausen, for their painstaking work on the project. Finally, special thanks to the long-standing mainspring of the *Schülerkreis*, Father Professor Dr. Stephan Otto Horn, S.D.S., who with unshakable calm makes the preparations for our meetings, obtains the Holy Father's approval, and organizes the events while carrying on and promoting communication among us. In consultation with the Holy Father, he also took on the whole burden of publishing these proceedings in collaboration with the Libreria Editrice Vaticana. May they become a positive milestone in the discussion about creation and evolution, which has lasted now for 150 years!

As a sign of our gratitude, the *Schülerkreis* has the privilege of presenting this book to the Holy Father as a little *Festschrift* in honor of his eightieth birthday.

† Christoph Cardinal Schönborn

PRESENTATIONS

The presentations published here were given on September 1, 2006, to the assembled Schülerkreis *and repeated on September 2 in the presence of Pope Benedict XVI. They were revised for publication.*

Peter Schuster

Evolution and Design
A Review of the State of the Art in
the Theory of Evolution

I

Preliminary Remarks

The present essay deals exclusively with the scientific aspects of biological evolution and therefore cannot make any statements about the philosophical or theological implications of the idea of evolution. As in every other branch of knowledge in the natural sciences, the concepts of biology are derived from the interpretation of empirical data, and present-day evolutionary theory is a conceptual construct that is not incompatible with those observations that can be interpreted. The most important mechanism of biological evolution is the Darwinian principle of optimization through variation and selection. There are also, however, some evolutionary processes in living nature that require other mechanisms to describe them (see section 10).

Present-day biology is a field that is undergoing rapid development. Like theories from other branches of the natural sciences, the mechanisms of biological evolution cannot satisfactorily describe all phenomena in detail. Molecular biology currently offers new insights into what takes place in the submicroscopic world. The incorporation of ever-new findings into biological theory leads to a dynamic

27

development of scientific ideas about what happens in living systems.

The way in which the Darwinian mechanism of optimization through variation and selection functions has been replicated in laboratory experiments, and these studies have shown that in test-tube experiments a fine-tuning of molecular "recognition" can be achieved, similar to that which otherwise has been observed only in natural molecules. Hence the theory of evolution is an empirically based and verifiable theory that holds in the natural sciences a position comparable to that of the various theories of physics, for example [Newtonian] mechanics, electrodynamics, or quantum mechanics. In the form of population genetics, the theory has even been formalized mathematically.

Scientific research into biological evolution is dedicated to two different inquiries that, in practice, should be considered separately. (a) The investigation of the mechanisms of evolution, which in principle can be made directly accessible to experimentation, looks for the physical and chemical causes of observed changes and if possible traces them back to known processes. (b) The scientific reconstruction of the origin and development of our present-day biosphere is a historical science that traditionally relies on paleontology and in the last fifty years has increasingly been able to refer to interpretations of the additional findings of molecular biology.

2

Darwin and Mendel

The Darwinian principle proceeds from three observations: (a) in the reproduction of living things, characteristics of the parents are transmitted to the offspring; (b) the organisms in a population are not all identical; in other words, there is a natural variation of their characteristics; and (c) in every ecosystem many more offspring are produced than can survive on the basis of the available resources. The variability is caused by continuous (immeasurably) small changes that can arise as a consequence of a not entirely perfect process of reproduction. From these three individual observations follows one simple conclusion: All characteristics that tend to increase the number of offspring[1] have a self-reinforcing effect. In other words, more offspring in the first subsequent generation have as a result even more offspring in the second subsequent generation, still more in the third, and so on. Since only a certain number of offspring in all can be fed, the most productive variety ultimately drives out all the others. Illustration 1 (on page 46) shows an impressive example: Although the two varieties differ only by 10 percent in their fertility (eleven offspring to every ten of the other), the relative composition of the population, starting with a proportion of 99:1 in favor of the less fertile variety, reverses after about 97 generations and then assumes the proportion of 1:99.

Interestingly enough, Charles Darwin's notions about heredity were completely wrong.[2] He believed in the heredity of acquired characteristics and did not distinguish between

[1] For the sake of simplicity, we use the term "offspring" for the average set of those offspring which in turn produce offspring for the next generation. In other words, sterile offspring and the set of those offspring that do not reach the age of reproduction are not taken into account. In biology, the expression "fitness" is commonly used to designate this criterion of fertility.

[2] The reference consulted for the information about the history of science in the nineteenth century that is used in this essay was: Michael Ruse, *The Darwinian Revolution* (Chicago: University of Chicago Press, 1979). Particulars about the biological points of view mentioned here can be found in

29

the germ line and somatic cells. This distinction was first made by August Weismann around the year 1900. Darwin's ideas, which have often been characterized as "pangenesis", proved to be incapable of accounting for the evidence and were definitively disproved, at the latest, by the findings of molecular biology. With respect to parental influences, in the later editions of his *Origin of Species* he assumed that inherited traits blended evenly. Units of inheritance (what is understood today by the term "genes") were foreign to his way of thinking. They would have contradicted the (immeasurably) small steps that, as the advocates of Darwin's theory of evolution supposed, controlled the changes. There were probably historical reasons for the stubborn insistence of nineteenth-century evolutionary biologists on this sort of gradualism: In the first place, Charles Darwin had been strongly influenced by the geologist Charles Lyell, who postulated slow processes in geology. In the second place, it seemed important to him to take a position clearly contrary to that of the naturalist and paleontologist Georges Cuvier and his followers, who considered catastrophes to be the sole cause for the discovery of no longer existing species in fossil finds.

The correct mechanism for biological heredity (see illustration 2, after page 60) was deduced by the Augustinian monk Gregor Mendel from his experiments with hybrid plants. Mendel had had a solid education in mathematics and physics, and therefore he was no stranger to statistical considerations. He was in a position to evaluate correctly the results of his experiments with plant pollination. The essence of Mendel's findings is simply this: Hereditary

Ulrich Kutschera, *Evolutionsbiologie*, 2nd ed. (Stuttgart: Verlag Eugen Ulmer, 2006).

characteristics are passed on, not by a "blending" of paternal and maternal traits, but rather in the form of "units of inheritance" [*Erbpaketen*]. For any particular unit there is a pair of "alleles", or alternative forms, one from each parent, contributed by the father and the mother from their respective pairs of alleles. At the time of his discoveries, Mendel's work attracted little notice.

Two different sorts of changes in genotype occur: (a) the "hereditary units" are recombined in different ways, thus resulting in new combinations with new characteristics for the carrier, and (b) changes are introduced in the individual units, and genuinely new alternative forms are generated. Today the name for these hereditary units is "genes", the changes are called mutations, and the term "allele" was introduced for the alternative forms. By their very nature, mutations are abrupt and can cause either minor or major changes in the characteristics of the carrier.

3

The Synthetic Theory of Evolution

From the beginning until the middle of the twentieth century, evolutionary theory and genetics were implacably at odds with regard to the importance of ongoing selection and abrupt mutations for the development of the biosphere. Although the population geneticists Ronald Fisher, J. S. B. Haldane, and Sewall Wright demonstrated as early as 1930 or so, using mathematical techniques, that genetics and natural selection can be reconciled without any problem, it was not until after World War II that the synthesis of Darwin's and Mendel's ideas was accomplished in the synthetic theory of evolutionary biology. This synthesis is connected with names such as Theodosius Dobzhansky, Ernst Mayr, Bernhard Rensch, and others. The synthetic theory[3] is by its very nature a macroscopic theory and is not based on molecular structures or other qualities of organic molecules, which at the time of its development were almost completely unknown. Two ideas are elements of the neo-Darwinian notion of evolutionary processes: (a) mutations or incidents of recombination are undirected, which means that they do not occur more frequently just because their carrier has an advantage and less often if they are detrimental to the carrier, and: (b) it appears that the expediency of changes and adaptations can be substantiated only a posteriori as a consequence of optimization through variation and natural selection. The concept of teleology is replaced by the new concept of "teleonomy". Purposefulness is only apparent and is not a prerequisite or a driving force of the evolutionary process, but rather its result.

This is illustrated, for example, by the beak formations of the "Darwinian finches". Through mutation and recombination, the "primordial Darwinian finch" has the natural tendency to develop a large number of different beak formations. Through a particular use—eating seeds or berries or insects—the variety having a beak formation suited to this use has an advantage and can ingest more food and thereby raise more offspring. In fact, the observation of the birds on the Galapagos Islands, on which the finches occupy various ecological niches, was an important contribution to Charles Darwin's knowledge as he formulated the principle of optimization through variation and natural selection. The

---

[3] Many evolutionary biologists include molecular biology as well in the "extended synthetic theory"; for the sake of greater clarity that should be avoided here.

spatial division of a population into sub-populations, like the one that resulted on the individual islands of the Galapagos Archipelago, plays the most important role in the development of species.[4]

4

What Distinguishes Biology from Physics and Chemistry?

The development of molecular biology began in the 1950s with the clarification of the molecular structures of the two most important classes of organic molecules, proteins and nucleic acids. Scientists were able to deduce the ways in which these macromolecules or organic polymers function from their spatial structure. Two classes of organic polymer molecules are especially important for the description of biological evolution: nucleic acids and proteins. Both are unbranched molecular chains with two chemically different ends. In their structure they can best be compared to strings of pearls. In nucleic acids we are dealing with four different sorts of pearls; in proteins, with twenty (illustration 3). The four letters of the nucleic acids are referred to as nucleotides, while the twenty building blocks of proteins are called amino acid residues. The chemical structure can be recorded in abbreviated form as a series of letters. This contains information about the spatial structure and the characteristics of the molecule in encoded form. The spatial structure of a

---

[4] The definition of biological species is based on their isolation in sexual reproduction: individuals from different species have no descendants capable of reproduction.

molecule results from the chain of letters as they coil or wind about in space.

Nucleic acids are found in two closely related classes:[5] deoxyribonucleic acid (DNA) and ribonucleic acid (RNA). In all cells the processing of the information encoded in the series of letters follows a one-way street in this direction:

$$DNA \rightarrow RNA \rightarrow protein.$$

The one exception is a class of viruses, the so-called retroviruses, in which the step RNA → DNA occurs also. Inside the cells, at chemical factories on a molecular scale, the chain of letters in RNA is translated into the sequence of building blocks in a protein, whereby a three-letter word of nucleic acid corresponds to one building block in the protein (illustration 4). The code controlling the translation is redundant—sixty-four three-letter words correspond to twenty amino-acid residues and one punctuation mark, "stop". This flow and processing of information provide the molecular basis for what is inherited genetically, and that is why we speak about genetic information and the genetic code.

The reproduction of cells (illustration 5) or organisms is, if compared to the kinetics of a chemical reaction, an autocatalytic or self-reinforcing process. If not restricted by limited resources, the number of individuals in a population would increase exponentially. Such self-reinforcing processes are also found in chemistry. In that field they give

[5] Both classes of nucleic acids consist of a basic framework or "backbone", to which individual (monomer) residues are attached at periodically occurring sites or loci. In RNA, the somewhat simpler molecule, the basic framework consists alternately of ribose and phosphate, and the purine and pyrimidine bases A, G, U, and C occur as residues. In DNA, instead of ribose there is 2-deoxyribose, and U is replaced by T.

rise to a whole series of phenomena such as pattern formation, oscillations, and even explosions. Autocatalysis in biology is distinguished from the corresponding process in chemistry by the transmission of information. Before every division of a cell, the genetic information in the form of DNA is duplicated and each of the two daughter cells receives one copy of this information. Biochemists call this duplication process replication: both DNA and RNA molecules can be replicated. In nature, RNA replication occurs in the reproduction of viruses. In laboratory experiments, RNA replication is the most important element for test-tube evolution. In the DNA molecule are stored complete building instructions for the duplication of a cell. This building plan comprises not only directions for the assembly of the proteins through the translation of the message that is stored in the nucleic acids, but also the directions for the construction of the translating mechanism. To put it metaphorically: Besides the directions for assembling an automobile, the plan for building the automobile factory is transmitted as well.

No copying process can go on with absolute precision. There will necessarily be "transcription errors" or mutations (illustration 6), which form one basis for the variation of organisms postulated by Charles Darwin.[6] Accordingly, mutations are changes in the sequence of letters in DNA. These mutations are passed on to the offspring, and therefore every organism carries within itself a record of its history. Therefore, by using suitable mathematical methods, the family tree of an individual or of a species can be worked out from differences in the DNA sequences (illustration 7).

[6] The other basis is furnished by the recombination of genetic information in sexual reproduction, during which, according to Mendel's laws of heredity, the paternal and maternal genotype is divided up and combined in a new way (illustration 2, see the color plates after p. 60).

For the sake of completeness, we should mention that besides genetic inheritance there is also an epigenetic transmission of characteristics, the molecular details of which have already been researched to a large extent today. The various epigenetic mechanisms determine, among other things, which genes are active in an organism, that is (as was explained above), are transcribed into RNA and translated into protein. One example of the consequences of epigenetic transmission is the fact that the harm caused by hereditary diseases differs in seriousness, depending on whether the defective gene was inherited from the mother or from the father.

5

Where Does Chance Come from, and What Role Does It Play in Biology?

The word "chance" is used for various sorts of happenings that are characterized by our incomplete insight into their causal connections. The lack of insight can be of a fundamental nature, as is the case with the information that is restricted by the lack of definition at the quantum mechanical level, or else it may be due to information that is incomplete or capable in principle of being supplemented. For practical purposes this distinction is often insignificant, because gaining complete knowledge about a state of affairs can be impossible for reasons related to the time allotted for the investigation or the capacity of the available mechanisms for collecting data. Here we intend to limit our discussion to the role of chance in biological evolution, and we will begin with the process of mutation.

As mentioned in the preceding section, transcription errors in copying genetic information are called mutations. They can be errors that affect only individual letters, and these are called point mutations. In so-called insertions, parts of the sequence are transcribed twice or even more times; in deletions, the transcription is incomplete and the copy contains one or more letters less than the original (illustration 6). Viewed in terms of the dynamics of a chemical reaction, correct replication and mutations are reactions that proceed in parallel, following precisely defined mechanisms. How, then, can chance find a way into evolutionary biology? The precision of the molecular copying processes is so great that, for example, in bacteria only one error occurs per one hundred million (100,000,000) letters. This means that, if there are three thousand characters on a page, a wrong letter occurs on average only once every 33,333 pages, which is the equivalent of one error in one hundred books, each containing more than three hundred pages. Replication has a high rate of precision, and consequently the occurrence of a particular mutation is a very rare event. We will illustrate this fact with a statistical example dealing with point mutations: The DNA of the bacterium *Escherichia* contains around four million letters; every nucleotide can, in the case of a mutation, be replaced by three other nucleotides, and thus for every DNA sequence there are potentially twelve million one-letter mutations. If all point mutations were equally probable,[7] then one or another mutation would appear on average every twenty-five replications, whereas a particular mutation would appear only once in three billion

[7] In reality, point mutations vary in frequency, but this fact is irrelevant to the general statement that we are trying to make here.

replications. In an infinitely large population all mutation processes would occur according to their frequency. In fact, however, both in nature and also in a laboratory experiment we are dealing only with a restricted number of individuals, and consequently during the period of observation only a few mutations appear. Which ones these will be, however, is not foreseeable, since the probabilities are too small for a meaningful statement. The impossibility of a complete description of all microscopic processes and the lack of a sufficiently large number of individual instances that have been observed result in a high component of chance in a mutation. This still does not take into account quantum phenomena, which can further increase the random character of the individual mutation.

The astronomer Fred Hoyle once used the following metaphor to illustrate the impossibility of an evolution leading to complex forms of life: Suppose that all the parts of a jet aircraft were lying around in a dump. A tornado sweeps through the junkyard, and finally the jumbo jet stands there, fully assembled. Is Hoyle right, or is he guilty of a fallacy? One can easily accuse him of such an error in reasoning: The metaphor is not pertinent, because in the case of the aircraft there is only one correct way of assembling it or only a few combinations of the parts that are fit for flight and thus display a flight advantage over the pile at the dump.

In the case of biological systems—whether they be individual organic molecules or entire organisms—there are, however, countless preliminary stages that in and of themselves can already be more functionally fit than their predecessors. This state of affairs can be illustrated best by means of another metaphor: Imagine an enormous golf course with a perfectly even lawn. The chance that a random stroke from the edge of the course will hit the hole in the middle is practically nil; this represents Hoyle's argument. But the landscape on which the ball is hit can also have quite different properties. For example, it can have the form of a funnel, along which the ball rolls toward the middle, and then every stroke from the edge lands precisely in the hole. Applying this to biology, the two landscapes, the golf course or the funnel, correspond to two extreme situations. In the case of the golf course, all variants are equally good or equally bad, with the target sequence as the only exception that optimally fulfills all the desired requirements. With the funnel landscape, every mutation along the way to the target sequence leads to an improvement and would therefore be selected by the Darwinian process of natural selection. It is difficult to determine the structure of the landscapes upon which evolution takes place in nature, but there is already a series of results for individual organic molecules. From these we can conclude that the natural landscapes display neither the form of a golf course nor that of a funnel. Evolutionary experiments in the laboratory have shown, however, that gradual optimization of molecular characteristics is in fact possible through a Darwinian process.

Even though the frequency of individual mutations is in no way related to their effect, natural selection brings about a direction in the evolutionary process. Those varieties are selected which have more offspring. In this respect, evolution corresponds to the often used Monte Carlo technique for optimization: Steps resulting from a random process are accepted only if they lead to an improvement in the solution. Experience teaches that optimization methods that build upon random steps are superior to conventional, deterministic methods in highly complex tasks.

6

Complex Behavior from Simple Rules

The natural world that surrounds us is of an extraordinary complexity, which extends from the chemistry of molecular events to the many leveled behavior of human beings in societies. An argument that had often been used, that complexity cannot arise from simple elements, has been refuted by simple mathematical structures called cellular automatons, which are reminiscent of board games. Cellular automatons generate patterns that are made up of occupied and unoccupied fields. The essential part of a cellular automaton is made up of the rules that allow one to calculate the configuration in the next time interval from the present configuration. Beginning with a starting configuration, dynamic structures are produced that can simulate purposeful behavior, among other things. An impressive example illustrating this is John Horton Conway's "Game of Life", which is played on an extended chessboard pattern. Since there are two independent directions along which the automaton can develop, it is classified as two-dimensional. Among the various simple dynamic patterns, the development of the "Gosper Glider Gun" is particularly impressive.[8] From a starting configuration, a dynamic pattern develops in about seventy time intervals that discharges small moving elements that occupy five squares, so-called "Gliders", in a precisely determined direction.

---

[8] Examples from Conway's *Game of Life* can be studied very easily: the software can be downloaded from an Internet link, http://www.bitstorm.org/gameoflife/, and any PC in the current generation is capable of displaying the individual dynamic patterns.

A few years ago Steven Wolfram suggested a classification of one-dimensional cellular automatons that lends itself to a definition of complex behavior. There are cellular automatons that after a few steps pass into a completely ordered state or simply oscillate between two or several patterns. The one-dimensional cellular automatons in another class exhibit no (discernible) periodicity in the patterns and are therefore described as chaotic.[9] Both the chaotic and the ordered systems have a simple repertoire of behavior. Wolfram identified, however, yet another, fourth class of one-dimensional cellular automatons, which after a starting phase appear neither ordered nor simply periodic nor chaotic. Indeed, they form complex patterns and have been viewed as an analogy to the complexity of living systems, which is expressed in the phrase, "Life at the edge of chaos".

Without trying to press the metaphor too far, we can declare that complex behavior can arise through the repeated application of very simple rules. Thus we are dealing with an example of the phenomenon of self-organization. The complex behavior is not contained completely in the rules or exclusively in the starting configurations, because complexity here is a product of the dynamics of the process.

7

The Genealogical Tree of Life

Charles Darwin already postulated that all living beings were produced from a primordial form of life. The relatedness of

[9] All cellular automatons with a finite extension, after a maximum number of steps that can be calculated, must either become periodic or else reach a static condition.

the organisms was diagnosed on the basis of their appearance, that is, through morphology. Until the second half of the twentieth century the morphological reconstruction of the genealogical tree of living things was the only information about the evolution of species. The sources of this information are both the life forms living today and also those that are extinct and preserved in fossils. Darwin was well aware of the importance of the existence of a genealogical tree for his theory of evolution: The sole illustration in his epoch-making book *On the Origin of Species* shows a genealogical tree that grows from a single root.

Cellular biology, which began in the second half of the nineteenth century and developed into a science through the use of the conventional microscope, demonstrated that all organisms are made up of cells. Therefore it was reasonable to look for a primordial form of the cells that are alive today. Decisive progress in the search for the common elements of all organisms was first made by molecular biology: the chemistry of life is expressed through molecular machinery, which with the help of several thousand genes—in higher organisms several tens of thousands—carries out cellular reproduction, and all the basic features of this machinery is the same in all living creatures.

The comparison of the genetic information of various organisms living today allows us to make direct conclusions about the degree of relationship between them and thus permits the reconstruction of their phylogeny. Our DNA and likewise the DNA molecules of all other living things are the result of a large number of individual mutations, which altered a "primordial DNA sequence". All organisms living today, accordingly, carry within them in the form of their DNA a "memory" of their past, which allows us to make unambiguous or merely vague statements, depending on the span of time that the analysis is supposed to bridge. A persuasive finding, if not the most convincing evidence of all, for the correctness of the theory of evolution is the fact that the phylogenetic tree based on morphology and the molecular-genetic family tree of life forms, with some exceptions, agree down to the most minute details. Since these two methods of reconstructing the history of life are independent of one another, they form the two legs on which current evolutionary biology stands and together make up its backbone.

8

Experiments in Evolution and Computer Simulations

Generally speaking, it is not possible to observe evolution directly, since the intervals between generations are too long. The only exceptions are bacteria, viruses, and RNA molecules. They can multiply so swiftly that the time intervals available for experimentation are sufficient for scientists to study natural selection and evolutionary adaptation. The selection of simple and constant environmental conditions makes it possible to distinguish clearly between evolutionary dynamics in the population and environmental influences. In a laboratory experiment it is possible at any time to take samples, and hence we obtain an uninterrupted record of the course of evolution. We will mention here only a few typical examples.

In 1988 Richard Lenski from the University of Michigan in East Lansing began an experiment, which is still continuing, on bacteria of the type called *Escherichia coli*, which he allowed to evolve under constant conditions. As of today he has isolated and analyzed around forty thousand generations. The three most important findings of this experiment in evolution under constant conditions are: (a) the bacteria evolve in clones that are more closely related to one another than to the rest of the population and form lines of development that resemble genealogical trees; (b) the number of mutations on the DNA level is proportional to the time that has elapsed and can vary greatly in different strains of bacteria; and (c) despite these continual changes in the genetic sequences, externally observable adaptations to the conditions in the artificial environment of the laboratory experiment take place in gradated steps.

Of the numerous evolutionary studies on viruses, and in particular phages,[10] we mention here only the one that was carried out by James Bull at the University of Texas in Austin. The object of the study was the bacteriophage $fX174$, which attacks bacteria of the type *Escherichia coli* as its preferred host. Its DNA is only 5,386 nucleotides long, and thus it has only a little more than one-thousandth of the genetic information of its host. It owes its survival to the fact that it uses the bacterium's genetic machinery and reprograms it for its own reproduction. In the laboratory experiment, James Bull and Holly Wichman allowed a population of phages to grow in a suspension of bacteria for 180 days. This span of time amounts to approximately thirteen thousand generations of phages. Besides a careful analysis of the mutations that occurred and of their effects on the virulence of the phages, the authors found evidence that the bacteria and their parasites were continually adapting to each

[10] Phages, or more precisely bacteriophages, are viruses that attack bacteria as their hosts. Because of their relative simplicity, phages were the most important system for systematic analyses in the early years of molecular biology.

44

other, as though in an "arms race". The environment of the phages is a constant one only on superficial inspection. In fact, co-evolution enters the picture, and this, as in nature, has no foreseeable end, unless one of the two partners loses its ability to adapt.

Evolution experiments with RNA molecules were carried out as early as the 1960s by Sol Spiegelman. He placed the RNA derived from the RNA-phage Q* into a medium that was suitable for the replication of phage-RNA and allowed it to multiply there. Such a medium contains all the building blocks necessary for the synthesis of phage-RNA, along with an enzyme that catalyzes the replication. After some time, when the medium had been used up, he transferred a small sample into a test tube with fresh medium for replication and repeated this procedure about one hundred times. This manner of proceeding, which is not dissimilar to the way experiments with bacteria are carried out, is called the "serial transfer method". The experimental series resulted in RNA molecules that multiplied much more quickly than the molecules at the start. Through competition within the population of molecules, those varieties were selected (compare illustration 1 on p. 46) that multiplied most quickly under the given conditions. Spiegelman's experiments were analyzed by Manfred Eigen and Christof Biebricher at the Max Planck Institute for Biophysical Chemistry in Göttingen, Germany, with the methods used to study the dynamics of chemical reactions; the result of their detailed investigation was that we know as much today about test-tube evolution as we do about most other common chemical processes. Evolution in the Darwinian sense is a universal phenomenon not bound to the existence of cellular life, and this was demonstrated by means of an example of biochemical

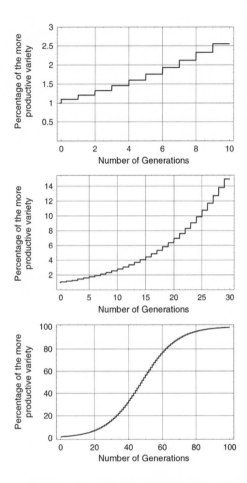

Illustration 1: Selection according to the Darwinian principle. In a population there are two varieties that differ by 10 percent in the average number of their offspring. Their fitness values were set at 10 and 11 respectively. The starting population of one hundred individuals contains the two varieties in the proportion of 99:1. The three charts differ only in the time scales. After a sufficiently large number of generations, the original stepwise function becomes a smooth curve. After about one hundred generations, the more productive variety has completely driven out its less successful competitors.

reactions.[11] The evolution of RNA molecules in laboratory systems has also been carried out according to artificial criteria of selection in much the same way as in breeding animals or plants. Thereby scientists have succeeded in "breeding" molecules that are tailor-made for predetermined functions. One of the most important results of these studies is the fact that, with simple methods that build upon the Darwinian principle, molecules are obtained that are not inferior to natural biopolymer molecules as far as their selectivity toward bonding partners and the multiplicity of their functions are concerned. Natural evolution and evolutionary design in laboratory experiments are currently in a position to achieve results that outshine any rational design[12] of biomolecules by biophysicists.

Computer simulations have also been conducted in order to obtain, experimentally, information about evolution in simple systems that is presently not accessible. In these studies, computer modeling was used to simulate the optimization or "breeding" of RNA molecules. The individual steps of the "serial transfer experiments" were replaced by the continuous system of a flow-reactor. The most important result is that these studies have clarified the cause of the gradated approach of the populations to the goal

[11] The experimental studies by Biebricher had been preceded by theoretical models and the mathematical analysis thereof; see, for example, the popular presentations by Eigen and Winkler, *Das Spiel* (Munich: Piper-Verlag, 1975), and by Eigen, Gardiner, Schuster, and Winkler-Oswatitsch, *Spektrum der Wissenschaften* 6 (1981): 37–56, as well as the somewhat more demanding presentation by Eigen and Schuster, *The Hypercycle: A Principle of Natural Self-Organization* (Berlin, Springer-Verlag, 1979).

[12] By rational design is meant the construction of biomolecules on the "drawing board", based on present knowledge of structural biology and biophysics. The classical "drawing board" of the engineer, of course, was replaced in this discipline, too, more than thirty years ago by computer simulation.

(illustration 8). Short successful sections are interrupted by long plateaus in which no discernible improvement takes place. Nevertheless, during the quasi-stationary periods, mutations of the RNA sequences can be observed constantly. These mutations have no influence on the fitness or in general upon the phenotype, which in this case is determined by the structure of the RNA molecule. Mutations that have no effect on natural selection are described as neutral mutations. An evolution that does not result in differences that are significant for natural selection affects only the sequences and has been described by the population geneticist Motoo Kimura as "neutral evolution". A typical statistical survey of the mutations that occur in natural populations of higher organisms indicates only a few advantageous new alleles as compared to large percentages of neutral and disadvantageous mutants. An analysis of the computer simulations shows that phases of successful optimization end when no more advantageous allele can be attained by a one-step mutation. The populations then grow, on the basis of the neutral mutations, until a neutral allele is found that can serve as the starting point for further optimization. The gradated structure of the course of optimization is caused by the fact that optimization driven by natural selection proceeds much faster than the "search" by the populations based on neutral mutations.

9

Time Scales of Evolution and External Influences

Evolution experiments with simple organisms or nucleic acid molecules have shown that evolutionary processes need not by any means take their course gradually. The data show that there are evidently two time scales of evolution: (a) a rapid one, which is determined by natural selection among the varieties having different degrees of fitness, and (b) a slow one, which is characterized by a constant average fitness of the population. The simplest interpretation of this state of affairs is that advantageous mutations are rare occurrences and that therefore a population must wait for a long time after the conclusion of a selection phase before a further advantageous mutation appears. The fact of the existence of a large number of neutral mutations refines the simple interpretation as follows: the two time scales are the result of phases of optimization, corresponding to processes of selection, and periods of a random or aimless wandering on the basis of the neutral alleles.

All the observations that have been described and the interpretations thereof are restricted to evolution under constant external conditions. This does not exist in nature, however, for several reasons: (a) as we have already mentioned in discussing evolution experiments with bacteriophages, there is such a thing as co-evolution, and (b) the world of living things is subject to fluctuating environmental conditions. For an individual species, the environmental conditions in a natural ecosystem are constantly being changed by co-evolution. The adaptation of one species leads to the continuous worsening of the living conditions of all other species, which can be counteracted only through their own further adaptation. This leads to an endless process of adaptation, which resembles the international arms race in human societies. If a species has reached the end of its possible adaptations, then it is eliminated by the ongoing development of the other species; its ecological niche becomes free and is immediately occupied by another species that is better prepared for further competition.

49

In Darwin's time, the theory of evolution and the hypothesis of catastrophic development brought on by climatic or extraterrestrial causes were irreconcilably and antagonistically opposed to each other. Today that scenario belongs to history: on the one hand, the theory of evolution is an established part of the natural sciences and does not need to engage in a "fight for survival", and, on the other hand, accumulating evidence indicates that global catastrophes did in fact take place. Scientists have found clear traces of the impacts of large meteorites, and among them the one that occurred at the Cretaceous-Tertiary boundary is the most popular, since it is supposed to have greatly accelerated the extinction of the dinosaurs, if it did not actually cause it. Another climatic catastrophe that is discussed is the Snowball-Earth hypothesis.[13] Today there is no doubt that the historical development of life on earth was shaped equally by eras of favorable climatic conditions and by phases of extremely bad living conditions, for example, ice ages and periods of drought or flooding.

10

The Major Transitions in Biological Evolution

The Darwinian mechanism of evolution can explain optimization, adaptation to an environment, and co-evolution

[13] By "Snowball-Earth" is meant a long geological era in the late Neo-Proterozoic, during which almost the entire earth was frozen over. This epoch is considered to be responsible for, among other things, the long duration of a world of prokaryotic one-celled life forms that had preceded the sudden onset and swift development of eukaryotes and later on of multi-celled life forms. Relevant literature can be found in Hoffman and Schlag, *Terra Nova* 14 (2002): 129–55, and Bodiselitsch, Koeberl, Master, and Reimold, *Science* 308:239–42.

understood as a sort of "arms race". In addition, however, there are also developmental phases in earthly life during which other mechanisms must have been and must be at work. The table on page 60 lists the eight most important major transitions.[14] The common feature of all these transitions is that a step up to a hierarchically higher level of complexity was made possible by a new characteristic. At the higher level, former competitors joined together in an organized unit. A conceptual model for the formation of functional units through the union of competitors was suggested as early as the 1970s. An essential element of these ideas is the development of modes of cooperation between competitors. No doubt the competitors must already have within themselves the capability of cooperation. For example, RNA molecules that are supposed to combine through mutual catalysis to make a new unit must bring along with them the ability to catalyze the relevant chemical processes. In fact, RNA molecules can efficiently catalyze a large number of different chemical reactions. In particular, catalytic RNA molecules, so-called ribozymes, were discovered that accelerate the division or the combination of other RNA molecules. Other modes of cooperation are exhibited in symbioses for the mutual benefit of the partners or in the collaboration of individuals in animal or human societies.

In illustration 9, the above-mentioned model for the formation of higher hierarchical units is depicted in four steps: (a) competitors join together through cooperation to form a network of mutual dependencies; (b) from this network

[14] John Maynard Smith and Eörs Szathmáry have described in minute detail the "major transitions" of biological evolution in a monograph: Maynard Smith and Szathmáry, *The Major Transitions in Evolution* (Oxford: W. H. Freeman, 1995).

arises an ordered functional unit that includes all the individuals involved in the catalysis; (c) the new unit develops a boundary over against the environment—membrane, skin, specific group recognition by means of pheromones,[15] rituals, or languages—to ward off parasites, and (d) the Darwinian mechanism starts again on the level of the higher hierarchical units. This model has been analyzed mathematically and confirmed by computer simulation; at present all that is lacking is a simple, manageable experimental system, analogous to the RNA replication by which we became acquainted with the simple Darwinian mechanism.

Presently the best known and most plausibly explained transition is the one from simple prokaryotic cells without nucleus to eukaryotic cells with a highly structured cellular organization consisting of nucleus and cell organelles.[16] Much evidence today points to the formation of the first eukaryotic cells through endosymbiosis, a process of integration that joins several formerly independent organisms into a single cell.[17]

Common to all of these modes of cooperation between former competitors is the fact that again and again there are single individuals that try to break out of the group to their own advantage. In order to prevent this, the group has to develop means of exercising control. In illustration 9, these non-cooperative individuals are labeled parasites. As indicated there, parasites not only must be excluded

[15] Pheromones are chemical substances that can be sensed in extremely rarefied form and cause very specific reactions. Especially well-known forms of pheromones that have been analyzed chemically are the substances involved in sexual attraction.

[16] Cell organelles of animal cells are the mitochondria that manage the production of chemical energy through oxidation. In plant cells there are, in addition, chloroplasts, which carry out photosynthesis.

[17] For further information on the endosymbionts theory of the origin of eukaryotic cells, see Kutschera, *Evolutionsbiologie*, 149ff.

from the formation of the cooperative group, but must also be rendered harmless if they arise within the group. This battle against individuals that lapse into a parasitic way of living runs through all of biological evolution: DNA segments that multiply independently from the rest of the DNA, as so-called "selfish genes", must be brought under control. Transformed cells that elude this control and multiply in an uncontrolled manner as tumors must be recognized by the immune system and eliminated in order to avoid the death of the organism through cancer, and criminal elements in a human society must be quarantined so as to prevent the disintegration of society. In this sense, the joining of individuals into a hierarchically higher and more complex group involves costs that must be paid in order to maintain cooperation. The benefit through synergies and new capabilities, however, must be greater than these costs, so that the new functional unit does not just disintegrate.

11

Evolutionary Tinkering and the Complexity of Organisms

An important feature of the evolution of the biosphere is manifested in the fact that all cells, from the simplest bacterial life forms to the most highly developed animals, including man, use almost exactly the same biochemical machinery. Otherwise it would not be possible, for example, for us to produce human proteins like insulin or erythropoietin in bacteria using gene technology. This also means, however, that the metabolic equipment of the cell, once set in motion, remained unchanged to this day, with the exception of marginal modifications.

53

In retrospect, it is evident that there were many switching points in the development of the biosphere that sent evolution down a track that increased fitness for survival in its day but proved to be an unalterable disadvantage for later development. By way of illustration we should mention here three examples drawn from the anatomy of vertebrates: (a) the nerve fibers in the vertebrate eye are conducted from the side of the retina that is turned toward the light, and hence the optic nerve has to pass through the retina, causing the so-called blind spot in our eyes; (b) the crossing of the air and food passages in the vertebrate larynx leads to all sorts of complications when breathing or speaking is attempted at the same time as eating or drinking, and (c) the restriction to four limbs does not permit the development of birds with both wings and hands.

In his collection of lectures published in 1982, François Jacob included a chapter with the title "Evolution and Tinkering",[18] in which he presents arguments showing that biological evolution works, not like an engineer who always thinks up a new design for the parts of his machines and sketches them on the drawing board, but rather like a tinker who makes his assemblages out of whatever parts happen to be around. The progressive deepening of our knowledge of microbiology has completely confirmed François Jacob's ideas. It would go beyond the parameters of this

---

[18] François Jacob, *The Actual and the Possible* (New York: Pantheon Books, 1982). "Tinkering" is translated into German as *Basteln* and into French by the term *bricolage*, which often connotes insignificant work or handicraft using inferior materials. In recent times, *bricolage* has been equated with the notion of a "do-it-yourself" job (DIY). A technical survey of evolution as a tinker can be found in: Duboule and Wilkins, "The Evolution of *Bricolage*", *Trends in Genetics* 14 (1998): 54–59.

essay to list all the interpretations of the data currently available, which clearly point toward the tinkering nature of the evolutionary process. As a typical example, we single out genome duplication. Reconstruction of the genealogical tree of organisms living today from data in their DNA sequences has shown not only that single genes were duplicated by insertions (illustration 6), but also that the duplication of the entire genome has often occurred. The best-researched case study involves brewer's yeast, *Saccharomyces cerevisiae*, the genome of which was duplicated about one hundred million years ago. Comparison of the DNA sequence of the yeast with that of an organism which at that time was closely related to it, *Kluyveromyces waltii*, resulted in proof of the genome duplication. Since as a rule there is no need for a second copy of a gene, over the course of time most of the doubled genes lost one copy. A few of the second copies of genes acquired new functions and in that way enlarged the repertoire of the organism's genetic-metabolic characteristics. Similar lines of reasoning have been presented for two duplications of the genome in vertebrates two hundred million years ago. Further genome duplications of a more recent date have been reported for frogs and fish. Strong indications of genome duplication are found with particular frequency in some phylogenetic plant lines.

As a result of gene or genome duplications, identical or very closely related molecules acquire two or more functions in an organism. One consequence of this is the need for more subtle regulatory mechanisms in order to prevent malfunctioning. As can easily be imagined, the regulatory and controlling functions become more and more complex through continued processes of this sort. Some biologists see in the increasing complexity of organisms over the course of evolution an effect of the tinkering principle. We should assume that several causes are responsible for the increase in complexity; the principle of new possibilities opening up through the doubling of available genetic material and variation of the unneeded duplicates is surely one of them.

Another point of view concerning the complexity of higher life forms will serve as our conclusion. We present here the evolutionary development of eyes as an example of evolution leading to a complex organ, which can be traced and analyzed on a molecular basis. Eyes are found in vertebrates, cephalopods, and insects, among other phyla. Conventional biology regarded these three organs of sight, along with the more primitive eyes of other organisms, as three independent evolutionary developments. More recent molecular genetic studies by Walter Gehring,[19] however, have shown that all known eyes have a common evolutionary origin: identical or closely related genes control the development of eyes in very different organisms. Furthermore, it seems that the common origin of all forms of eyes is to be found in a single light-sensitive molecule, which first appeared long ago and can be dated back to the primitive life forms of the early Precambrian Era or even earlier. One interesting detail about the three highly developed eyes mentioned above involves the manner in which the light-sensitive cells are connected with the neurons. In two instances, in cephalopods and insects, evolution

[19] In many original studies, Walter Gehring from the Biocenter [*Biozentrum*] of the University of Basel has investigated the molecular genetics of the development of eyes. Two summaries of his research have been published in Gehring, "The Genetic Control of Eye Development and Its Implications for the Evolution of the Various Eye-Types", *International Journal of Developmental Biology* 46:65–73, and *Zoology* 194 (2002): 171–83.

produced a technically correct arrangement: the neurons leave the light-sensitive cells on the side of the retina turned away from the incidence of light. In one instance, as was already mentioned above, the nerve fibers leave the retina on the wrong side—on the side on which the light falls—and, since the bundle of nerves has to be conducted through the retina to the brain, a blind spot results in our eyes. Now, if in the case of our highly complex eyes an evolutionary path leads from one cell with a light-sensitive pigment to the perfect organ, then it is not difficult to imagine that this path was determined by continual improvements. To possess a light-sensitive cell, after all, is an advantage over an organism that cannot tell where the light is coming from.

Reverence and awe are called for with respect to the outcome of evolutionary tinkering. The "Do-It-Yourself" principle (DIY) of biological self-organization has in fact brought forth astonishing results. Although in many details the solutions obviously could be improved upon, we must admit that there is no known chemical system that uses and manages light and energy better than the cell, that among all mechanical robots and other human artifacts there is no construct that moves more economically and elegantly than animals with their limbs, or that among all the computer-driven pattern-recognition programs there is not one that can seriously compete with the human brain in its ability to recognize. Perhaps the superiority of nature consists in the fact that she optimizes wherever the costs are not too high, but where the expense begins to surpass the benefit, she gets along with solutions that are just fit enough to function. Proteins and other biomolecules are generally optimized for their respective functions, but higher organisms are not: they are—only—fit for survival.

12

Summary and Concluding Remarks

According to the current state of our knowledge, prebiological and biological evolution, from the first molecules capable of multiplication to the human being, appears to be a whole. We recognize that it is a process that goes on according to natural laws and needs no external intervention. Furthermore, the natural scientist at present is making not one single observation that could be explained compellingly only by the interference of a supernatural being, nor is one necessary for the extrapolation of our present knowledge to the interpretation of events in the past. Obviously and, because of "Occam's razor", inescapably, it is the assumption of evolutionary biology that such an intervention, should it occur or have occurred, cannot be the object of scientific speculation. From our colleagues in the fields of astrophysics and cosmology we learn of similar interpretations of the development of the cosmos down to the formation of our earth. The development from the Big Bang down to the human being and eventually farther seems to be a unified cosmic process.

In this final paragraph I would like to deviate a little after all from my stated intention of writing only about natural science and add a personal remark. What fascinates and moves me is the relatively narrow corridor in the multiplicity of all possible worlds through which the path leads from the beginning of scientific ideas about the Big Bang to the present cosmos. My friends who are cosmologists tell me that a small change in the natural constants would result in completely different worlds. The prebiological or chemical evolution upon earth requires a rather narrow range of tem-

peratures, and the development of the biosphere, understood as biological evolution from the original formation
of life down to the human being, passed through a considerable number of "needle's eyes", which were determined
by climatic and other adverse environmental conditions. The
successful interplay of these many conditions seems to me
utterly remarkable, and it is here, I could well imagine, rather
than through interventions in the course of biological evolution, that there would be room for a bridge to be built
between theology and natural science.

Replicating molecules	*Membranes, organized partitioning* →	Molecules in compartments
Independent replicators	*Molecular chains, joint replication* →	Chromosomes
RNA as a gene and an enzyme	*Genetic code, ribosome* →	DNA and protein
Prokaryotes	*Union through endosymbiosis* →	Eukaryotes
Asexual reproduction (cloning)	*Origin of sexual reproduction* →	Populations that reproduce sexually
Protists	*Cell differentiation and development* →	Plants, fungi, and animals
Individuals living alone	*Development of non-reproducing castes* →	Animal colonies
Primate societies	*Language, writing, culture . . .* →	Human societies

Table: The Major Transitions in Biological Evolution. The new characteristics that make possible the transition to a more complex life form are printed in each case in italics over the arrow.

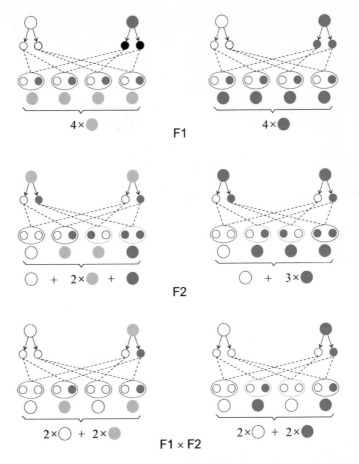

F1

4 × 🔴   4 × 🔴

F2

⚪ + 2 × 🔴 + 🔴   ⚪ + 3 × 🔴

F1 × F2

2 × ⚪ + 2 × 🔴   2 × ⚪ + 2 × 🔴

Pair of Intermediary Alleles   Pair of Dominant/Recessive Alleles

Illustration 2: Rules of Mendelian heredity. All organisms possess two samples of (almost) all their genes. The "genome" is divided up into individual genes before the formation of offspring, and the alternative forms (alleles) are combined at random from the "gene pool". At the molecular level this process takes place through a reduction division (meiosis), whereby a recombination of genes becomes possible. Mendel's laws result in proportions among the varieties, which are understood today as approximations, analogous to limiting cases. Two different types of genes are distinguished: (a) the intermediary type, which [is expressed] in the mixed genotypes that carry one each of the two different alleles—such "heterozygotes" are depicted here by the color pink as an intermediate color between white and red, and (b) the dominant/recessive type, in which the heterozygote exhibits the same phenotype as the homozygote of the dominant allele.

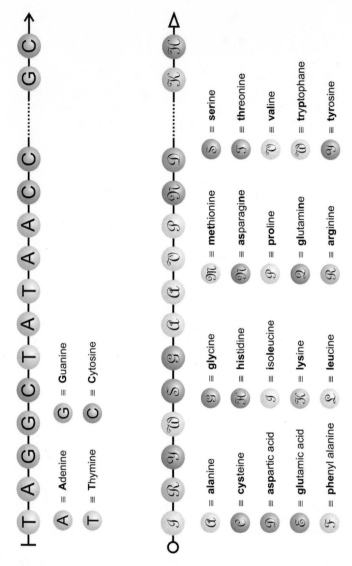

Illustration 3: Schematic structure and classes of the chemical building blocks of nucleic acids and proteins. The color code for the nucleic acids: purine bases—yellow-green and orange; pyrimidine bases—blue and red-violet; pairings of bases: yellow-green with blue, and orange with red-violet. For the proteins: hydrophobic amino acids—yellow; polar amino acids—blue; positively charged amino acids—yellow-green; and negatively charged amino acids—red-violet.

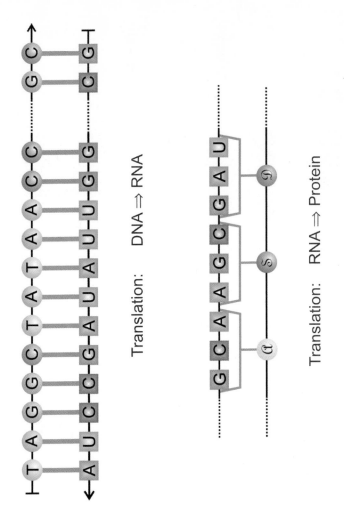

Illustration 4: The processing of genetic information in cells. Cellular DNA is transcribed piecemeal into RNA. In this process, as in replication, the complementarity of the nucleotides among the Watson-Crick bases is employed, ensuring that there is no ambiguity: A=U(T) and G=C. In RNA the nucleic base uracil has the same function as thymine in DNA. In the translation of a nucleotide sequence into a protein sequence, the genetic code is applied: three nucleotide bases correspond to one amino acid residue. Transcription is carried out by highly specific enzymes, so-called RNA polymerases, whereas for translation the cell possesses highly complex, minute granules, ribosomes, which in general are made up of three RNA molecules and fifty-five protein molecules.

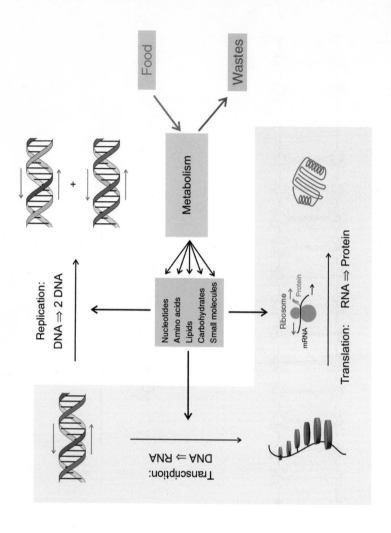

Illustration 5: Cellular metabolism from a molecular-biological perspective.   In order for the cell to multiply DNA, all the necessary materials must be synthesized by a highly complex metabolic network of chemical reactions. The metabolism is propelled by a chemical flow, Food → Wastes. Concerning transcription and translation, see illustration 4.

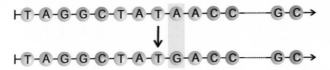

Point mutation

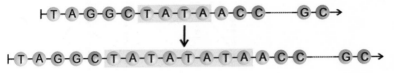

Insertion

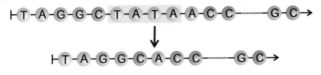

Deletion

Illustration 6: Categories of mutations. In point mutations, a nucleotide is copied incorrectly. The frequencies of the twelve possible errors of this sort are different. In insertions, a segment on the DNA is copied twice (or several times). In the case of a deletion, a segment is omitted.

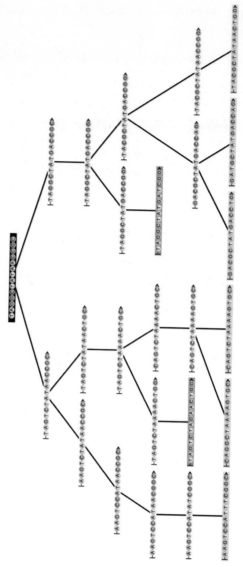

Illustration 7: Reconstruction of genealogical trees of biological evolution from molecular data. From a comparison of the DNA sequences of organisms living today, a genealogical tree of the species can be reconstructed, since every organism carries within it a record of its evolutionary past in the form of a temporal series of mutations that have been accumulated and passed on by heredity.

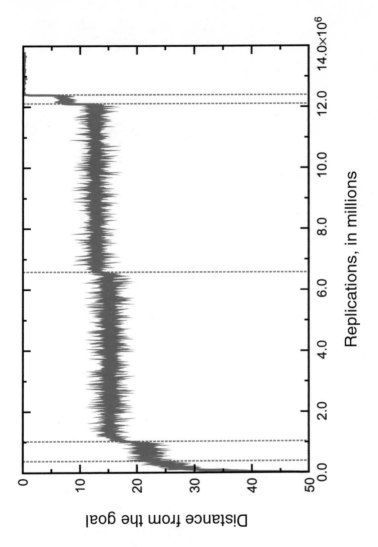

Illustration 8: Computer simulation of an optimization according to the Darwinian mechanism. The blue curve traces the mean distance of a population of three thousand molecules from the target structure that they are supposed to reach. In the neighborhood of the replication numbers indicated with red dotted lines, there is rapid progress in optimization, whereas on the long plateaus between them there is no sign of improvement. Nevertheless, the population is accumulating so-called neutral mutations that, while bringing it no closer to the goal, still lead to variants from which further optimization is possible.

Level I:
Independent replicators
in competition

Level II:
Catalysis and competition
during replication

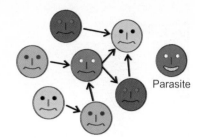

Parasite

Level III:
Functionally connected
replicators

Parasite

Level IV:
New unit of selection

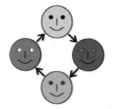

Parasite

Level V:
Independent units in
competition

Illustration 9: A model for macroevolutionary steps. Four logical steps lead from one level of complexity to the next higher level: (a) the elimination of competition through mutual support in the form of catalysis or symbiosis, (b) the formation of a functional unit by cyclical catalysis, (c) demarcation from the environment, so as to be able to keep parasites from exploiting the newly formed unit, and (d) the reintroduction of Darwinian optimization through mutation and selection at the hierarchically higher level.

Robert Spaemann

Common Descent and Intelligent Design

The biologist Rupert Riedl is the author of a book entitled *Die Spaltung des Weltbildes* [The rift in our world view]. By this Riedl meant two ways of looking at things: the perspective of the natural sciences and that of the humanities. His book proposed to overcome this division. He intended to overcome it by integrating man's understanding of himself into a biological view that was supposed to be capable of behaving integrally and not antithetically toward this self-understanding and, thus, of explaining it biologically, that is, functionally. The rift in our world view is old. The first systematic reflection upon it was by Leibniz, who as the inventor of infinitesimal calculus immediately noticed that with the help of this method we can for the first time make mathematical calculations about movement by dissecting movement into an infinite series of stationary positions. Yet as a philosopher, he saw clearly that precisely the motive character of motion is thereby lost. For this reason, Leibniz introduced in his metaphysics the concept of *conatus*, the concept of something like a tendency, an impulse, which means that every body in motion is defined at every moment by the anticipation of a future position. We know what that means from our own experience of ourselves. We know what it means to be out for something. If we do not act on this experience, then we cannot understand something like movement and must simply and flatly deny its existence, as the Eleatics did. Leibniz did not try to overcome the rift in our world view; rather, he regarded it as unavoidable for finite beings. In this connection he spoke about the two kingdoms, the *regnum potentiae* [the kingdom of power] and the *regnum sapientiae* [the kingdom of wisdom]. Leibniz was not only a natural scientist and a humanist; he was a philosopher. Philosophy is not one of the humanities; rather, it is the attempt to understand what is at the basis of this dualism. All attempts thus far to integrate the two ways of seeing into one single perspective have not reached their goal. They are still reductive. Either the natural sciences felt that their claims were not being taken seriously, or else people found that their elementary experiences were not being explained but rather explained away. The eighteenth-century German poet Friedrich Schiller admonished the natural scientists and philosophers of his time:

Feindschaft sei zwischen euch, noch kommt das Bündnis zu frühe.
Wenn ihr im Suchen euch trennt, wird erst die Wahrheit erkannt.
[Let there be enmity between you; for agreement it is still too early.
Only if you separate while searching will be truth be known.]

It seems to me that it is still too early today, just as presumably it will be impossible in every age, to determine the position and the momentum of a subatomic particle. Even more illusory will always be the attempt to have the theory of the hypercycle in mind and simultaneously to suppose that that theory is a state or condition of one's own brain. But it is completely absurd to think that someday we will be able to deduce theories or a mathematical equation from our observation of a cerebral state, whereby this state itself would have to be described in turn as a cerebral state. The remark by David Hume, "We never do one step beyond ourselves", could be formulated only by someone who has already taken such a step.

What does this mean for the question about the need for the *regnum potentiae* of Darwinian theory to be supplemented by a *regnum sapientiae*, in which there is talk of something like a "design"? Does the interplay of random mutation and natural selection explain for us who we are and how we became what we are? And what does "explain" mean here? When is something explained? When have we understood it? Here, too, we are dealing with two fundamentally different approaches. What do we understand better: the life of the amoeba or the bacterium, or the highly complex life of the human being? If "to understand a thing" means "to know what we can do with it when we have it", as Thomas Hobbes once said, if it means, therefore, being able to reconstruct and simulate the thing, then the bacterium is more comprehensible than the human being. Normally, however, we think that we better understand what we ourselves are than what a bacterium is. Indeed, we will never know what it is like to be a bacterium or a bat. If I see a bat eating, then I assume that it is hungry. And what it means for a bat to be hungry, I can only understand by a distant analogy to my own hunger. For my own hunger is hunger that is aware of itself, which presumably the bat's hunger is not. But if I become aware of my own hunger, then I am conscious of it as something that does not come into being just at the moment of that awareness. And that unconscious hunger cannot be something in principle completely different from the hunger of my dog when he runs to his food dish. If there were not a relationship here, then nobody would ever own a dog.

Biology does not deny this relationship. It emphasizes it. But when it speaks about life, it does not start with the highest paradigm, the one most immediately accessible to us, namely, our own experience, but rather with the phenomena that are farthest from us and have a certain degree of complexity. These are supposedly understood when we can reconstruct them, and that means: simulate them.

The perfect simulation would be identical with the original, because the original itself is nothing other than its own simulation. The subjective experience of life as being-out-for-something, however, is an addition, which itself in its systemic function can again be explained in evolutionary terms. But what can be explained here is only the selective advantage of subjectivity, not its origin. Words like "fulguration", "emergence", and so on, are, after all, only words for the appearance of something new that—and this is precisely the point—cannot be derived from the old state of affairs. We can call this new thing inwardness, and, more particularly, inwardness at first in the form of an instinct. Non-living systems have no instinct; they are not out for anything. Tendencies of non-living systems to maintain and reproduce themselves are only interpreted as tendencies by us, the observers, that is, by analogy to our own being-out-for self-preservation. Real being-out-for is essentially not something objective for the observer, but rather it is an initial form of subjectivity. One characteristic feature of genuinely teleological phenomena is that there are mistakes and errors with reference to them. (Here I would like to contradict Cardinal Schönborn, who wishes to attribute mistakes only to free beings. If a rabbit is born with only one leg, then it is, as Aristotle correctly says, a matter of a *hamartia tes physeos*, a mistake of nature.) In the world of physics there are no mistakes except for those made by a theory.

But wherever there is instinct, the discrepancy with what is factual begins. There is pain, there is frustration and error, and there is desire, joy, satisfaction.

To generalize, we can say that there is negativity. Negativity, however, cannot be constructed out of positivity, out of facticity. Of course, we can introduce a minus sign, which is a positive fact in the world, exactly like a plus sign. But we cannot derive its meaning from what is factual. Just as in mathematics we can construct the plus sign with the help of the minus sign—negative times negative is positive—while positive times positive is always positive again. We must already have introduced the minus in order to transform plus into minus with its help. A smart bomb does not aim to reach its target; its builder does. The category of teleology cannot be derived from an ateleological reality. It is in principle something new. But allowing this new thing to come about only with human consciousness, as many theorists of science do, contradicts our intuition based on immediate evidence. Obviously animals are out for something, although we cannot see their being-out-for-something itself, because it belongs to their subjectivity. Cartesian scientists in the seventeenth century logically denied the phenomenon of pain in animals, because they considered inwardness to exist only in the form of self-consciousness. Teleological explanations do not compete with causal explanations. They just allow us to understand why causal series interact in such a way that the result of their interference is a meaningful figure. Of course, this interference, too, can be by chance. If we dump letters out of a bag onto the ground and the result is the Prologue to the Gospel of John, that can be by chance. Every combination is possible and just as probable as any other. But—with all due respect to Occam's razor—in such a case no one would believe it was chance; everyone would look for the trick. The trick in evolution is natural selection, which by means of the hypercycle drastically reduces the improbability of certain configurations, namely, those that are useful for survival and multiplication. But natural selection can only favor something that is already there. It is not a creative principle that explains the development of something absolutely and categorically new, of what I, following Hegel, am calling negativity. The configuration of the Prologue to John's Gospel can in fact be by chance. That means that it can be indifferent to the meaning of this text. This combination of letters becomes a text only in the head of the reader. But it is quite different with the development of that sort of meaning on the basis of which we read this configuration *as* a text. Here an emancipation from all conditions for development takes place. It is obvious that the appearance of sense and meaning, and therefore of life, is bound up with a particular sort of high complexity of matter. But what appears then is not complexity, but rather something absolutely simple: inwardness. Life is not a state of matter; rather, it is the being of a living thing. *Vivere viventibus est esse* (For living things, to live is to be). And that is true again to an even higher degree where negativity emerges in the thought of the other as the other who does not only belong to my world but to whose world I belong, and in such a way that I know it. And it is true wherever the idea of something unconditional appears, which by definition is *not* defined by its function in the context of preservation. That is to say, in aesthetic, moral, and religious contexts. When Professor Schuster calls what happens in natural processes "beautiful", he is using a predicate that belongs to another world than that of biology. The biologist will not rest until he has discovered the biological basis for this predicate, too. But in doing so, he will not have explained the predicate.

Allow me to make two remarks in conclusion.

1. If we are unwilling to abandon either science or our human self-understanding, then we have to affirm the dualism of the two world views. There are prerequisite conditions for the development of life, of instinct, of consciousness, and of self-consciousness. But prerequisite conditions are not sufficient causes. They do not explain for us who we are. Being oneself is emancipation from the prerequisite conditions. Every attempt to overcome the dualism idealistically or materialistically, that is, through the reduction of the one side to the other, will leave the subsumed side unsatisfied. Someone who wants to affirm the unity of reality without surrendering one of the two sides can do this only if he brings the idea of creation into play; according to this idea, the process of the natural development of life and of the species of living things, including man, is founded upon the same will of a Divine Wisdom that also wills the result of this process, namely, a natural being that discovers its natural origin and thanks the Creator for his life, that is, for his existence. The same Bible that speaks about the fellowship of all that is living, with which God enters into a covenant, says that God himself lives and that this life is the light of men. And therefore that life precedes the matter that it animates. For anyone who is unable or unwilling to take this step, the only possibility remaining is to say with Gottfried Benn:

> Ich habe mich oft gefragt und keine Antwort gefunden
> woher das Sanfte und das Gute kommt,
> weiß es auch jetzt noch nicht
> und muß nun gehn.

[I have often asked myself, and found no answer,
where kindness and goodness come from;
even now I still do not know
and now I must go.]

2. The second remark is this: Material configurations can be carriers of coded information. Information for a being that can understand something *as* something—in other words, can perceive meaning. The fact that information about a functioning system is sufficient to enable us to understand the development of the material structure says nothing about whether there might not be a second code that contains a completely different message. The objection that Occam's razor forbids us to make such an assumption, since it is superfluous to an explanation of the structure, has only limited force. A Creator with unlimited power is not subject to Occam's razor. Even Johann Sebastian Bach was not subject to it. Some years ago a double code was discovered in the G-minor Violin Sonata by Bach. If we follow a particular cabalistic system that during the Baroque period was called *geomantia*, in which musical notes, letters, and time values are arranged in a definite order, then we find encoded in this sonata the following text: "Ex Deo nascimur, in Christo morimur, per Spiritum Sanctum reviviscimus" (We are born of God, in Christ we die, through the Holy Spirit we come to life again). The sonata is a marvelous piece of music. The musicality of its configurations of notes is certainly reason enough for us to understand why Bach composed it. However if someone, following a rumor, suspects that something else could still be hidden here and makes the attempt to search for a further message, and that person has mastered Latin, then suddenly a further, unexpected dimension of this music appears before

his eyes. Fortunately a scholar investigated the case, and she did not allow herself to be intimidated by Occam's razor. But back to our topic: once someone has the dimensions of the unconditional at his disposal, and the old rumor about a Creator God keeps haunting him, he will not be intimidated if natural science hopes to find in functionality for survival the sufficient cause for the development of the natural species, including man, and to some extent has already found it. Wherever he encounters the good, the beautiful, and the holy, or wherever he encounters the truth claim of a scientific theory, he will discover a message that has been encoded in a completely different way, which by no means can be traced back to the first, although even the first one has its own beauty. But where the beautiful comes from and what it means that something is beautiful: this he will understand only with the help of the second message.

Father Paul Erbrich, S.J.

The Problem of Creation and Evolution

In the debate about creation and evolution very often an important distinction is not made clear, or else is not made clear enough, namely, between the fact of evolution and the cause or *causes* of the evolution, which is made out to be a fact.

Let us understand "evolution" to mean a continuous line of descent from the first organisms down to and including man. Apart from the development of recent varieties and breeds, no one has been able to observe directly and investigate such a connection. It has been deduced from evidence. The quantity of the evidence has constantly increased over the last two hundred years (along with the types of evidence). Simultaneously the span of time over which the multi-celled, higher organisms developed has grown to more than five hundred million years.

For these reasons the vast majority of biologists are convinced of an evolution encompassing all living things. For them it is more than merely a hypothesis, if for no other reason than because of the fruitfulness of the idea of evolution for research. The enormous quantity of biological facts becomes really comprehensible, meaningful, coherent, and consistent in the eyes of biologists only in light of the idea of evolution.

Whether the hypothesis of evolution—or, in less minimalist terms, the idea of evolution—can correctly be called a theory about which there can no longer be any reasonable doubt depends on whether the complex of sufficient causes that brought about evolution and keeps it going has really been recognized and proved.

Here is an illustration of this connection between fact and cause:

Between 1912 and 1915 the meteorologist and geophysicist *Alfred Wegener* developed the idea of continental drift. He gathered evidence that in his eyes indicated that the continents travel about on a viscous substratum, the outer mantle of the earth. Thus two hundred million years ago the Atlantic Ocean did not yet exist; it came into being only later, because the American double continent started to drift toward the west.

Hardly any geologists of that time bought this idea of his. Why? Because no plausible *cause* for such drifting could be specified. Where, then, is the force that would be capable of setting the enormous mass of these gigantic plates in motion and, then, of overcoming the enormous friction on the hard or viscous substratum that would result?

By the end of the 1960s practically all geologists were convinced of the fact of continental drift. Why? In the previous two decades scientists had gradually discovered the causes that could bring about the drifting apart and also the colliding of the continental plates on the earth's surface. Now many geological riddles were solved. Like a jigsaw puzzle they fit together into a grand, unified picture of plate tectonics.

Back to evolution:

I

Probably most biologists today are convinced that the decisive cause of the alleged evolution has been found. It is Darwin's mechanism of *chance* and *natural selection*, supplemented by the findings of population genetics. This mechanism may not be the sole cause, but it is the fundamental and decisive one. It came into effect at latest after the development of the first organism or organisms and is still in force.

Many biologists cannot understand how anyone can be for evolution and at the same time against Darwin's evolutionary mechanism. For them, this mechanism of chance and natural selection is inseparably linked with the fact of evolution. They take it quite for granted that whoever says Yes to evolution also says Yes to Darwin's mechanism. And anyone who calls this mechanism into question *eo ipso* also calls the fact of evolution into question and must be a creationist who assumes, at least about the first specimens produced from the fundamental blueprints, that one day they appeared fully formed on the fresh meadow, sniffed each other, and then stepped right up to reproduce.

Conversely, many critics of the theory of evolution cannot understand how biologists can credit so much to chance, even if they have no problems with the fact of evolution. Furthermore they not infrequently take exception to the expression "mechanism".

When the critics do this, they ought to make it unmistakably clear and admit that Darwin's mechanism is effective in their view also, but only as a mechanism of optimization. This, however, presupposes something to be optimized, which in turn cannot be in every respect simply the result of an earlier optimization but constitutes an innovation that must have come about in some other way.

Biologists have investigated the natural selection factor in the most minute detail. There are whole libraries on the subject. Remarkably, in doing so they often overlook the fact that selection presupposes purposefulness in the living things that are to be selected. The living things must "want" something. If they want nothing, if they pursue no goals (such as self-preservation or reproduction, for example), then there is no competition, either, no fight for limited resources.

But if there is no competition and no contest, there is no selection of the more successful. Snow packs that adhere to mountain slopes want nothing; they have no needs, no goals, apart from the fact that they "would like" to lie in ravines with low potential energy. It is all the same to them whether they rush downhill as avalanches or melt on the slopes in the spring. Among the different snow packs there is no competition and no selection. They invent no devices by which to reduce the friction between them and the substratum so that they will finally get their chance to rush downhill before the nearby competitor does.

There are by far fewer investigations, if any at all, into the "chance" in the expression "chance variations", or simply into "chance". Most often biologists speak as though everyone understood what is meant by chance. Chance, for biologists, seems to mean ultimately: arbitrary causes, first these, then those, but in any case always the absence of any sort of plan or design, of any goal-oriented activity and intention. This is considered to be downright axiomatic. Biology is supposed to remain free of teleology, as a computer is supposed to remain virus-free.

And where scientists can hardly do without "goal-oriented activity", it becomes mechanized as teleo-nomy in contrast to teleo-logy. This means that living things certainly do pursue goals, but only in the manner in which target-seeking antiaircraft defense missiles do. They do not really pursue; they only *simulate* pursuit. We know that antiaircraft missiles only simulate pursuit because we built them. We know that living things really pursue goals, because we, too, are living things and experience ourselves as beings who pursue things, sometimes even before we consciously set goals for ourselves. For the critics, in contrast, "chance" means an event for which sufficient efficient causes are to be found, but never final causes.

When Jacques Monod's Dr. Dupont is fatally struck on his way to a sick call by a hammer that slipped away from a roofer who was working up above, it is (from a this-worldly perspective) obvious to everyone that it is by chance. The efficient causes are plainly in view: the inertia of the hammer, the gravitational force of the earth, the limited solidity of Dr. Dupont's skull, and so on. We can hardly speak about a final cause. The hammer may tend toward a state in which it has the least potential energy, as all matter does. It has no tendency of any sort whatsoever to smash skulls; nor did the roofer have the intention of killing passersby.

For critics of the theory of evolution, however, it is obvious that evolution as a whole is goal-oriented, with an unheard-of stubbornness. For phylogenesis is an orthogenesis, a development toward a higher level, and not merely a constant, aimless, meandering modification of what has come to be thus far. It is not merely a question of an increasingly better adaptation to the environment. On the contrary, it is a question of an ever greater *emancipation* from the constraints of the environment, certainly not for every species of living thing, but for the front-runners in the evolutionary crowd.

What does this emancipation look like?

- Fish crawl onto dry land and, having become amphibians, are emancipated from water. This emancipation is still incomplete. Frogs and salamanders still have to go through their developmental phase in the water, and once on land they usually require constantly moist surroundings.

74

- But the slightly higher reptiles conquer the dry land, indeed, even the desert, by packing the sea in which their ancestors lived into their eggs, which they equip with a protective layer so as to prevent evaporation, but in such a way that the exchange of gases is not hindered. They acquire more efficient lungs, because now they are no longer capable of additional respiration through a moist skin. Sheer innovations, for which there were no prototypes before. Reptiles have already achieved the maximum emancipation from water; it cannot go any farther, because water is indispensable for life. One cannot be emancipated from water itself.
- Then the reptiles and mammals conquer the third dimension. They no longer crawl with their bellies on the ground in order to move forward, as lizards do. They get up on their legs and learn to walk like elephants or to run like cheetahs. They climb up trees like iguanas, squirrels, and apes, or they even soar through the air like the birds, descendants of the reptiles.
- All the warm regions of land have now been conquered, but not the cold ones. In order to emancipate themselves from warm surroundings, the mammals and the birds invent an inner oven that produces the required warmth. Now they can conquer even the icy wilderness, like the polar bear, and the icy seas, like the whales and seals.
- The pinnacle of this emancipation from the constraints of the environment is reached in man. The human being becomes capable of truth, that is, he does not merely recognize what appears, he can recognize (even if far from always and everywhere) what is or what possibly can be. There is no surpassing this, for what higher thing can anyone recognize than what is real? The same can be said about the ability to determine oneself, and not simply to be compelled by causes, in doing things or leaving them undone,

but rather to be lured by reasons that one can discern, affirm, or reject. To surpass this is hardly possible, although there is probably immense room for improvement (optimization) as well as for deformation in both faculties. And both of them have been running ever since man existed.

Emancipation, higher development, goal-oriented behavior, wherever you look. But if there is purposefulness, then there is no more compulsion to keep appealing to chance.

II

"Chance" is the first stumbling block; "mechanism" is the second. If you read articles by experts in *Nature* or *Science*, in practically every article you run into the expression "mechanism", especially in technical articles about biology, but also in those about geology and chemistry, and less often in those about physics. What the biologists, geologists, and chemists are looking for are mechanisms, not laws of nature. The laws of nature are supplied by the physicists. Laws of nature serve only to ascertain that a proposed or conjectured mechanism is possible in the first place. And so, for instance, no one seriously suggests a "perpetual motion mechanism" any more in order to solve a problem. For that contradicts the principles of thermodynamics.

But what is a mechanism? Actually the theorists of science ought to give us information about that. They, however, usually discuss the term only from a historical perspective as a fundamental program of natural philosophy to explain natural phenomena *causally* as the movement of bodies, by means of the classical mechanics of the seventeenth century (thrust and impact), and later with the additional help of long-range forces (Newton's gravitation, Maxwell's electromagnetism). With the advent of the theory of relativity and quantum mechanics, however, mechanisms are said to have become antiquated. The theorists of science have not noticed that they are currently of the utmost interest among researchers.[1]

Well, then, what is a mechanism? A term for causality that even today is widespread, especially in those branches of the natural sciences which cannot be expressed completely in mathematical formulae. A world in which mechanisms are the sole causality is a uniform, causally closed system. The causal closure of the world is widely accepted as a certain scientific finding, with the consequence that the body-soul problem becomes insoluble. There is no available room left for mental causality.

Mechanisms know of no centers of spontaneity in which new material chains of causality arise without the precursors that the laws of nature would require, and other causal chains end without the continuation that the laws of nature would lead one to expect. There is, however, one exception: the "spontaneous" resistance of real things to any change of their momentum, that is to say, of the state of uniformly rectilinear movement or rest that they have assumed by chance. We are talking about inertia, which Newton calls a *vis insita* [intrinsic force]. Since it is *insita*, it is a kind of spontaneity. This resistance can be changed only by *external forces* (*viribus impressis*, in Newton's phrase). Thus mechanisms always say who (or what) works *upon* whom in what

---

[1] On this subject, see the article "Mechanismus" in the *Handbuch wissenschaftstheoretischer Begriffe*, by J. Speck, ed., vol. 2 (Göttingen: Vandenhoeck and Ruprecht, 1980). Or in the *Enzyklopädie Philosophie und Wissenschaftstheorie*, ed. J. Mittelstraß, vol. 2 (Mannheim: Bibliographisches Institut, 1984). Compare, however, *The Philosophy of Science: An Encyclopedia*, ed. S. Sarkar and J. Pfeifer, vol. 1 (New York and London: Routledge, 2006).

way and with what consequences. The electrical charge of an electron does not help it to move itself; rather it helps to move another electron and then *to be moved* in turn by it.

What could tempt an observer to speak about mechanisms with reference to living things as well are the seemingly artful [*technikartigen*] structures of the organisms and the processes connected with them. Organisms are crammed with structures of this sort, starting from the macroscopic, through the microscopic, and down to the macromolecular level. They lead us to compare biology with human technology [*Technik*]. It is not surprising, therefore, that for a long time there has been a discipline within the natural sciences called bionics: *bio*logy plus tech*nique*. It attempts to understand structures and processes in living things by means of the principles and methods of technology and, vice versa, to mine the insights thus gained for ideas about how to improve human technology.

The common element in biological and human technology is that both of them outsmart the laws of nature with the help of the laws of nature. Thus it is possible to lift 400 tons with 800 passengers to an altitude of 10,000 meters and to make them hurtle through the air at 800 kilometers per hour, without the thing falling to the ground like a stone. Thus it is possible for green plants to reduce water and CO_2 with the help of light at room temperatures and not in the furnace heat of 1000° C and more, as in human technology.

III

If you want to give a short and clear description of technical objects, you indicate the purpose that they serve. Someone with technical understanding can read off this purpose from the structures without having to ask the builder what his purpose was. Technical structures are therefore rightly called "purposeful".

Now it is striking that purposeful structure occurs only in the realm of living things, in the biosphere. All human technology belongs to this realm also. Outside of and independent of life there is not a single trace of purposefulness; at most there is usefulness for the demands of the biosphere.

It was once thought that the maximum density of water at $+4°$ C instead of at $0°$ was a sort of purposeful property of water, namely, *so that* the oceans and seas would not freeze down to the bottom in the winter, which would have made higher life forms impossible. Today we know that this peculiarity is an unavoidable consequence of the strong polarization of the water molecule. No one is tempted to say that the two unequal orbits (2s and 2p) in the outer electron shell of the carbon atom unexpectedly become four equal q-orbits at the corners of a tetrahedron for the purpose of making carbon quaternary. This is merely the consequence of the laws of quantum mechanics. No one is tempted to say that the sun acquired that much mass *so that* it would eventually produce core temperatures of twenty million degrees Centigrade, making possible the fusion of atomic nuclei. The actual mass of the sun depends only on the mass of the dust and gases in the immediate surroundings of the developing sun, which was able to attract and incorporate them. If those masses had been by chance considerably smaller, a brown dwarf would have resulted; or a blue giant, had they been considerably larger. In the first case, the sun would long since have been extinguished; in the second case, it would have exploded before the planets could have formed. Between these two there are any number of intermediate possibilities.

The difference between a domain *with* purposeful, "artful" structures and a domain *without* structures of this sort is one of the most momentous differences in our cosmos. This is a leap that must give every evolutionary theorist butterflies in his stomach. For evolution seems *per definitionem* to presuppose a smooth curve that ascends, descends, oscillates, or describes whatever the pattern may be, for instance, the path of a satellite that falls to earth in an ever-narrowing spiral. Or if perhaps the evolutionary curve is not smooth, but rather composed of discrete steps, then these would have to be as small as possible, with no large leaps.

What to do? We change the word game! Scientists do not speak of purposefulness but rather of complexity. Complexity is found everywhere, even in the realm of inanimate things. The earth's climatic system, for example, is enormously complex, and so too are climate models. Gigantic computers that are supposed to simulate a hundred years of global climate with the help of such models chug along for weeks at a time in order to complete the task. The fact that living things, indeed, even bacteria, are complex does not have to be emphasized. But complexity admits of degrees, and the leap disappears.

Purposefulness, in contrast, like pregnancy, admits of no degrees. Within the realm of the purposeful, however, there certainly are degrees. There are highly complex purposeful structures and also others that are quite plain and simple. If one consistently speaks only about complexity, the ominous leap disappears, and the evolutionary theorists can breathe easily, for the time being at any rate.

One advantage of this change in the word game is that one can avoid the word "purposeful". For that smacks of teleology—but only of static teleology, actually, which is not dangerous after all. For purposeful or "functional" things as such and in themselves do not strive; they have no interests or needs. The purpose of the eye is not a goal that the eye itself would pursue—no dynamic teleology here. Its purpose is ultimately the purpose of the living thing that wants to see with its eyes. Besides, God as the designer, if he should exist, is still completely hidden. It may be that to affirm the existence of purposefulness *implies* someone who sets the purpose, but it does not *presuppose* him. The proof that there are purposeful structures, in and of itself, leaves entirely open the question as to what caused or produced these structures.

But if the aforementioned leap cannot be spirited away, then it follows that in the organic realm causes must be operative that do not exist in the inorganic realm—causes of a sort that is neither physical nor chemical, and thus any consistently reductionist attempt to explain them must be hopeless.

In the realm of inorganic, non-living things, everything—whether an atom or a galaxy—strives, if it strives at all, for the dead point of thermodynamic equilibrium that is attainable under the given circumstances (there can be obstacles along this path, for example, potential troughs or energy streams). The dead points are spatially and temporally different for different inorganic entities, but they are of the same kind, namely, dead points that, once reached, are impossible to leave unless compelled from without.

It is quite different in the organic realm. Living things strive away from the dead point and toward specific goals, of which there are incalculably many in an enormous variety. They do this with a gigantic arsenal of purposeful, "artful" structures and processes, some of which they inherit from their parents, but most of which they construct themselves during their lives (during ontogenesis) with the goal of resisting the tide of entropy and reaching the specific goal in each case: the organism capable of reproduction.

IV

But what, now, is this new cause that is required? Many biologists believe that they have found it in what they call the ability of complex material systems to *self-organize*.[2] But what is that? A reader who wrote a letter to the editor of *Nature* once opined that the concept would be very welcome and extremely helpful, if we only knew the *mechanism* of the self-organization! That is classic scientific thinking.

When a new concept crops up, it is a good idea to go back to the literal meaning of the words: organization of the self. The "self" is plainly the whole of the system under observation. Are we dealing here with an objective genitive or a subjective genitive?

- In the first case, the self, the whole, *is* organized. By what? By the complex interactions of the elements in the system. The "self" stands at the end of the process of self-organization as the result of these interactions. The whole is, if we can put it this way, a *"subsequent* totality".
- In the second case, the "self" organizes itself. It is a question of self-unfolding (according to the motto, "Become what you are"). The whole is present from the very beginning as an active potency, equipped with a toolbox, the zygote (fertilized egg cell), by means of which the "self"

[2] Not to be confused with "self-assembly", for example, the assembly of protein molecules into four-part structures based on the corresponding geometry of the surfaces of the subordinate units. An example: two proteins α and β resembling myoglobin, taken twice, combine to form one hemoglobin molecule.

builds for itself a body with all its molecular and physiological machinery, which with increasing maturity becomes something like a self-running appliance. Through this body the self creates for itself, in form and behavior, an unmistakable expression in space and enters into relation with its spatial environment, especially with life forms of its own kind. In contrast to the first case, the self stands at the beginning as the *original* totality, not at the end.

If this reflection should prove to be right, that would have a surprising consequence: A really original totality could not come into being through composition. For that would make it a subsequent totality. The fertilization, the fusion of an egg cell with a sperm, would not be the origin and first cause of a living thing; rather, it would be something like a *conditio sine qua non* [an essential prerequisite]. If not through composition, then what? Through a new foundation in a radical sense. The beginning of an original totality with its active potencies would be a moment of the creation of the world from nothing, a moment in the *one* creative act of God. Creation would be something that is still happening all the time and more than just an act of maintaining things in existence (*concursus divinus*).[3]

---

[3] The famous crippled cosmologist Stephen Hawking touched on this divine act of creation in passing when he expressed the opinion that a "theory of everything" (TOE), if there should ever be such a thing, would allow us—on the drawing board, so to speak—to derive all the properties of the elementary particles, the natural constants, and laws of nature from a priori mathematical insights. Of course then we would still not know whether what we thought up for ourselves as the only possible world really exists as well. To stay with this metaphor: We would have to get up from the drawing board and look out the window in order to see whether the made-up world exists, too. But then the question of where its existence comes from is unavoidable. See Stephen Hawking, *A Brief History of Time* (New York: Bantam Dell Publishing Group, 1988), 168f., 174.

Christoph Cardinal Schönborn

Fides, Ratio, Scientia
The Debate about Evolution

In 1686 Isaac Newton completed his *Philosophiae Naturalis Principia Mathematica*, which was published in London the following year. Newton added a *Scholium Generale* to the second edition in 1713. One of Newton's chief concerns in his *Principia* was to refute Descartes' theory of planetary movements, which he rejected as a materialistic theory. Newton writes that the perfection and the regularity of these movements cannot originate in "mere mechanical causes".

Rather, it is true that

> This most beautiful system (elegantissima haecce ... compages) of the sun, planets, and comets could only proceed from the counsel and dominion of an intelligent and powerful Being (non nisi consilio et dominio entis intelligentis et potentis oriri potuit). And if the fixed stars are the centers of other like systems, these, being formed by the like wise counsel (simili consilio constructa), must be all subject to the dominion of One (suberunt *Unius* dominio).... [A]nd lest the systems of the fixed stars should, by their gravity, fall on each other, he hath placed those systems at immense distances from one another. This Being governs all things, not as the soul of the world, but as Lord over all (ut universorum dominus).

But can we know him, who "on account of His dominion ... is wont to be called *Lord God Pantokrator*, or *Universal*

Ruler"? We have no idea, no notion of his substance, his essence. "We know him only [by his properties and attributes (per proprietates ejus et attributa), as well as] by His most wise and excellent contrivances of things, and final causes [of the world] (per sapientissimas et optimas structuras et causas finales); we admire Him for His perfections (et admiramur ob perfectiones)."

And in order to make these statements still more clear and decisive, Newton adds a vehement critique of deism (that is, the reduction of God's work to the activity of a "clockmaker" who is present only at the beginning), which even then was all the rage:

> A god without dominion, providence, and final causes (deus sine dominio, providentia et causis finalibus), is nothing else but Fate and Nature (nihil aliud est quam fatum et natura). Blind metaphysical necessity (a caeca necessitate metaphysica), which is certainly the same always and everywhere, could produce no variety of things (nulla oritur rerum variatio). All that diversity of natural things which we find suited to different times and places could arise from nothing but the ideas and will of a Being necessarily existing (tota rerum conditarum pro locis ac temporibus diversitas, ab ideis et voluntate entis necessario existentis solummodo oriri potuit).

He concludes this section of the *Scholium Generale* with a lapidary remark: "And thus much concerning God; to discourse of whom from the appearances of things, does certainly belong to Natural Philosophy (et haec de deo, de quo utique ex phaenomenis disserere, ad philosophiam naturalem pertinet)." [1]

[1] Isaac Newton, *Philosophiae naturalis principia mathematica*, 3rd ed. (London, 1726), 526–29. English ed.: *Sir Isaac Newton's Mathematical Principles of Natural Philosophy and His System of the World*, translated into English by Andrew

Newton's famous *scholion* [Greek: marginal comment] contains *in nuce* [Latin: in a nutshell] the essential questions that are still at issue today when people discuss the relation between science, reason, and faith. The emotion with which the debate is conducted was revealed once again when on July 7, 2005, I published an article on the subject in *The New York Times*.

Why have these questions been discussed since the days of Galileo and Newton with so much earnestness, with so much passion? There have always been disputes among scholars, and there always will be. The debate about whether or not a newly discovered manuscript contains an authentic work by Saint Augustine concerns a small circle of initiates. In contrast, the question of whether the universe and our planet Earth and we human beings owe our emergence to "blind fate" or to "an extremely wise and good plan" affects many people, because it involves questions that every human being asks himself sooner or later: "Where do we come from? Where are we going? What is the meaning of life?"

But should not these questions be posed to religion first? Does it make sense to expect answers to them from (natural) science? Is that not asking too much of science? But what if scientists, on the basis of their investigation of nature, come to the conclusion that everything can be explained as the result of a blind play of chance and necessity? Does the religious answer to man's primordial questions not then become groundless, baseless, a free-floating cantilever that without reason or foundation maintains that there is a meaning, a plan behind it all and that everything also has an

Motte in 1729. Translations revised and supplied with an historical and explanatory appendix by Florian Cajore (Berkeley: University of California Press, 1960), 79–80.

ultimate objective that God has willed and that he also realizes? Furthermore, if the claim that the world is evidence of a plan, of a purpose determined by the Creator, were proved scientifically to be untenable, then a belief in a Creator and his providence would also be *unreasonable*. Then belief in creation could be based at most on a *credo quia absurdum* (I believe because it is absurd). Yet a belief that builds on an absurd foundation is no belief, but rather an illusion. Is the belief in a Creator an illusion without a future, as Sigmund Freud, for one, tried to demonstrate?

Newton's *Scholium Generale* is part of this debate. For him the symmetry and regularity of the planets' orbits is a phenomenon that cannot be explained by "mere mechanical causes". This "most elegant" system can have arisen *only* through the counsel and dominion of a supreme intelligence. From natural phenomena we arrive at certainty about the Creator.

Is there, then, a "cosmological proof of the existence of God"? Do not many especially complex phenomena speak clearly in favor of an "intelligent design" in nature? Newton goes farther: Out of the blind play of chance and necessity the diversity of natural things cannot arise. The theory of evolution that is current today says precisely the opposite: Living species in all their diversity arose from the undirected play of the forces of mutation and selection. For Newton, all the diversity of natural things arose solely and exclusively from "the ideas and will" of the Supreme Being. And for him that is a certainty that he derives from his research. Or is it secretly the reverse: that his belief in the Creator makes him see things in this light? For the moment let us leave the question open.

First let us recount the famous anecdote that Voltaire popularized: Newton sat one evening on his parents' farm beneath an apple tree. "An apple fell from it. Newton saw this and looked at the moon that was shining in the evening sky. At that moment he asked himself the decisive question: 'If the apple falls to the earth, why doesn't the moon fall, too?' After all, the gravity with which the earth brings the apple down to itself must have an effect just as well on the moon—which indeed is farther away yet still within reach of the earth." [2] Now the moon does not fall on the earth. If it stood still, that would happen. But since it moves uniformly, it would move away from the earth without the latter's gravity. Both forces work together, the movement of the moon and the gravity of the earth. [3] Newton calculated this interplay of forces. He was convinced, however, that these regular movements could not have arisen out of mechanical causes, but "only from the counsel" and dominion of an extremely intelligent being, which we call God.

Newton assumed, moreover, that God's providence intervened again and again in order to ensure the stability of the planets' orbits and of the solar system. [4] Without such a repeated special intervention of the Creator, the order of the planets' orbits seemed inexplicable.

Leibniz objected that, according to Newton's doctrine, "God Almighty wants [that is, needs] to wind up his watch from time to time; otherwise it would cease to move"; in Newton's view, he said, God's work is "so imperfect ... that he is obliged to clean it now and then by an extraordinary concourse, and even to mend it, as a clockmaker mends his work." Leibniz considered that to be a debasement

[2] R. Taschner, *Das Unendliche: Mathematiker ringen um einen Begriff*, 2nd ed. (Berlin and Heidelberg, 2006), 52.

[3] See ibid., 53.

[4] See Stanley Jaki, *Intelligent Design?* (Port Huron, Mich.: Real View Books, 2005), 12.

of God's omnipotence and countered it with his own doctrine of the "beautiful, preestablished order" in which alone the wisdom and might of God is manifested.[5] To this day the question has lost none of its relevance. Does the Creator appear at all in his work?

Not even a hundred years later, when *Laplace* was quite able to give a "mechanical" explanation for the planets' orbits, he answered Napoleon, who uneasily asked him about God's place in this explanation, with the famous remark, "Je n'ai pas besoin de cette hypothèse" (I have no need of that hypothesis).

When God is supposed to fill in the gaps in man's knowledge, then his place becomes more negligible with each discovery that has managed to explain another bit of what was formerly inexplicable. These "survival niches" of the Creator became smaller and smaller, and the more successes the natural sciences had, the more certain of victory many in the "scientific community" became, claiming that the "God hypothesis" will someday be quite unnecessary.

Charles Darwin, too, took his stand upon this premise. As Professor Stanley L. Jaki has copiously and very precisely documented, Darwin was "possessed" by his determination to give a scientific, plausible explanation for the origin of species that could dispense entirely with particular, separate creative acts of God. His "theory of common descent", which only later was called the theory of evolution, was one long argument for a purely "this-worldly", indeed, a purely material, mechanical explanation for the "origin of species". Whereas Newton still said that from

---

[5] See *The Leibniz-Clarke Correspondence, 1715–1716*, ed. H. G. Alexander (New York: Barnes and Noble, 1956), 11–12. See also E. Dellian, *Die Rehabilitierung des Galileo Galilei oder Wie die Wahrheit zu messen ist* (privately published in Berlin, 2006), 326.

blind necessity no change and thus no diversity of things can arise, since that can result only from divine ideas and the divine will, Darwin said the opposite: The species in all their diversity have their origin in random mutations and in their chances for survival. For that no special interventions of the Creator are needed.

According to the thoroughgoing research of Stanley Jaki, very little doubt remains that with his scientific theory Darwin wanted to help bring about the victory of materialism. In the nineteenth century, God knows, he was not alone in this effort. It is no coincidence that Karl Marx and Friedrich Engels enthusiastically greeted Darwin's theory as a scientific foundation for their own theory.

Darwin's theory became a world view; this ideological component is probably also the main reason why, to this day, the discussion and the battle over evolution and creation continues with undiminished emotional intensity. The debate in recent months has clearly demonstrated this again. Therefore I consider it to be of the highest priority to bring more clarity into the debate by means of *natural philosophy*. This requires several steps:

1. Where is real science at work in Darwin's theory (and in its further developments), and where is it a matter of ideological elements that are foreign to science? We have to release Darwin from Darwinism, free him from the ideological fetters. There are good reasons to assume that that is possible.

2. It must be permissible to make an objective critique of the ideological sides of Darwinism. It is incomprehensible why it should be forbidden (so the debate is framed in the United States) to raise the God question in science lessons in public schools, whereas no one ever asks whether materialism (a highly debatable world view) may actually

be taught along with Darwin's theory. That does not have to happen, as long as biology instruction is not overloaded with ideological elements that are foreign to the subject. It often happens de facto, to the detriment of science, reason, and faith.

3. This demands, furthermore, great freedom in discussing the *open* questions in the theory of evolution. Often in the "scientific community" any question about the *scientific* weak points of the theory are blocked off in advance. What prevails here, to some extent, is the sort of censorship that people used to like to accuse the Church of practicing.

4. The decisive question, however, is found, not on the level of the natural sciences or on that of theology, but between the two: on the level of *natural philosophy*. I am more and more convinced that the decisive progress in the debate about the theory of evolution will be made on the level of natural philosophy, indeed, ultimately on that of metaphysics. It will do us all good to enter somewhat more accurately into the philosophical context of our debate.

5. For the debate in recent months has shown me one thing very clearly: It is an oversimplification, indeed, a caricature to reduce everything to a conflict between evolutionists and creationists. In doing that, we make the matter too easy for ourselves. The "creationist" position is based on an understanding of the Bible that the Catholic Church does not share. The first page of the Bible is not a cosmological treatise about the development of the world in six solar days. The Bible does not teach us "how the heavens go, but how to go to heaven".[6]

---

[6] Stanley Jaki, *Darwin's Design* (Port Huron, Mich.: Real View Books, 2006), 4.

The possibility that the Creator also makes use of the instrument of evolution is admissible for the Catholic faith. The question, though, is whether evolutionism (as an ideological concept) is compatible with the belief in a Creator. This question presupposes, again, that a distinction is made between the scientific theory of evolution and the ideological or philosophical interpretations thereof. That, in turn, assumes that we arrive at a clarification of the intellectual, philosophical presuppositions of the entire evolution debate.

Are belief in creation and the theory of evolution compatible? "Concordism", an opinion that is widespread nowadays, claims "that theology and the theory of evolution can *never* come into conflict, because the two disciplines move about in two completely separate realms." [7] This relationship, referred to by Stephen Gould as the NOMA principle (Non-Overlapping MAgisteria), is in my opinion untenable. There must be "intersections" between theology and the natural sciences, between believing, thinking, and investigating. Belief in a Creator, in his plan, his "rule over the earth", his guidance of the world to a destination set by him, *cannot* remain without points of contact with the concrete exploration of the world. Therefore it is true that not every variation on the theory of evolution is consistent with faith in creation.

Adrian Walker of the John Paul II Institute in Washington, D.C., comments: "A textbook example for such a problematic variety of evolutionary theory is what I call *strict Darwinism*: the thesis that the interplay of (genetic) mutation and natural selection is a *sufficient* explanation for the

<hr/>

[7] Adrian Walker, "Schöpfung und Evolution: Jenseits des Konkordismus" (Creation and evolution: Beyond concordism), *Internazionale Katholische Zeitschrift Communio* 35 (2006): 55–70, citation at 55.

development of new forms of life. For if mutation and selection *are sufficient* to explain this development, there is actually no reason why blind matter could not be the first origin of life—a thesis that . . . is incompatible with the Christian doctrine of creation." [8]

Often people look for a way out of this dilemma by saying that biology, or the natural sciences in general, are only *methodologically* materialistic, without therefore paying homage to materialism as a world view. Even if that were so, it is nevertheless clear that this *methodological option* is an *intellectual act* that presupposes reason, will, and freedom. That alone is already enough to show that the restriction of the scientific method to purely material processes cannot do justice to the whole of reality.

Newton's remark is true now as ever: It is the task of natural philosophy to make statements about God *ex phaenomenis*, starting from natural phenomena. The Catholic faith, together with the Bible of the Old and New Testaments, firmly maintains that reason can know with certainty the existence of the Creator from his traces in creation, although perhaps not without difficulty.

What, then, can reason know? First of all, that it exists and that it is more than its material prerequisites.

Allow me to elucidate this with a striking anecdotal example.

Late in his career, the German-American-Jewish philosopher Hans Jonas wrote an important work on the "ethics of responsibility" (*The Imperative of Responsibility: In Search of an Ethics for the Technological Age*). As he did so, it was clear to him that there is no sense in speaking about ethics and responsibility if there is no mind, no soul, no reason,

---

[8] Ibid.

and no free will. Genes assume no responsibility. Nor are they put on trial when they produce cancer cells. Nor are animals called to account. Only human beings bear responsibility and must (at the latest before the judgment seat of God) render an accounting for what they have done. Everyday living is a constant refutation of materialism. In business, for example, I must take responsibility. Bees and ants accomplish incredible things, but their behavior is guided by instinct, which is why they, too, are not responsible for their mistakes. Only free beings are responsible for their mistakes. Although everyday living constantly refutes the materialistic view, even very clever men fall into that error. Hans Jonas decided, therefore, to preface his "ethics of responsibility" with a philosophical refutation of materialism. He called the small book *Impotence or Power of Subjectivity?* It starts with the following anecdote: Three young scientists, all of whom were to become famous scholars, met in 1845 in Berlin and "pledged with a solemn oath that they would establish and compel acceptance of this truth: 'No other forces than the common physical chemical ones are active within the organism.'" The three men practiced lifelong fidelity to their "vow". Hans Jonas comments: "In the mere fact of a vow, they credited something totally *non*-physical, their relation to *truth*, with just that *power* over their overt behavior which the *content* of their vow on principle denied." [9]

What force is at work here? To be able to promise something, to make an effort to keep the promise, while running the risk of possibly breaking it, too: all this cannot be

[9] Hans Jonas, "Impotence or Power of Subjectivity". In *Imperative of Responsibility: In Search of an Ethics for the Technological Age*, trans. Hans Jonas with the collaboration of David Herr (Chicago: University of Chicago Press, 1984), 205–31, citation at 205.

the effect of forces that are of a purely material sort. The development of a scientific theory is an intellectual process, even if the theory is materialistic. Alfred North Whitehead's ironic remark about those Darwinists who rejected any and all purposefulness in nature is well known: "Those who devote themselves to the purpose of proving that there is no purpose constitute an interesting subject for study." [10] A human being experiences himself as someone who sets purposes and goals. Human activity is quite unthinkable in any other way than as goal-oriented activity. There is practically no example of activity that is more goal-oriented than scientific activity, and especially work in the natural sciences.

But how are things in the infrahuman world? How are things with animals, with plants, in inorganic nature, in the cosmos itself? Are there purposes there? If so, who sets them? Who pursues goals when there is no will that determines to do so? That is probably the key question in the debate about creation and evolution. A remark by Darwin in a letter to J. Hooker dated 1870 can help us along here: "I cannot look at the universe as a result of blind chance. Yet I can see no evidence of beneficent design, or indeed any design of any kind, in the detail." [11]

The observation of nature, the investigation of the universe, of the earth, of life speaks to us with "overwhelming evidence" (so I put it in *The New York Times*) of order, plan, fine-tuning, intention, and purpose. The question, though, is: Who recognizes the design? And *how* is it recognized? Darwin says that in the details of research into

[10] Alfred North Whitehead, *The Function of Reason* (1929; Boston: Beacon Press, 1969), 12.

[11] *More Letters of Charles Darwin*, ed. F. Darwin and A. C. Seward, 2nd ed. (New York and London: D. Appleton and Co., 1900), 1:321.

nature he can discern no design of any kind. With the strictly scientific, quantitative method of measurement that will probably not be possible, either. Martin Rhonheimer comments: "What we can in fact see and observe in nature are not plans or an intention, but at most ... the product thereof. We see teleology, goal-oriented activities, and an ordering of nature that is purposeful and also beautiful. Whether 'intentions' and 'intelligent design' are in fact the principle at work in these natural processes is something we cannot *observe*. What we see in nature is not design, but rather something that must be based on design." [12]

Of course, we constantly say that "nature" arranged this in this way, organized that in that way, and so on, as though "nature" were a subject endowed with intellect that sets goals for itself and acts to achieve them. Even strict Darwinists speak, yes, Darwin himself speaks again and again in this "anthropomorphic" way about nature, even though they then correct themselves and say, like Julian Huxley, for instance: "At first sight the biological sector seems full of purpose. Organisms are built as if purposely designed.... But as the genius of Darwin showed, the purpose is only an apparent one." [13]

Does "Nature" act as though she had goals? Saint Thomas Aquinas, in his *quinta via*, the fifth of his "proofs of God's existence", has pointed out an intellectual path in this regard that leads farther. Natural bodies (that is, corporeal things), he says, which have no intelligence themselves, act, as we

[12] Martin Rhonheimer, *Pro Manuscripto*, 4. These excerpts from a letter to the author have meanwhile been published as: "Neodarwinistische Evolutionstheorie, Intelligent Design und die Frage nach dem Schöpfer: Aus einem Schreiben an Kardinal Christoph Schönborn", *Imago Hominis* 14 (2007), vol. 1.

[13] Julian Huxley, *Evolution in Action* (New York: Harper, 1953), 7.

can see, in a goal-oriented manner to attain what is good for them. They achieve their end, not by chance, but intentionally (non a casu, sed ex intentione). But they achieve it, not by their *own* intention, for they have no intelligence, but rather through an intellect that directs them toward their end, as the archer directs his arrow. We call this intellect, which directs all natural things to their end, God (*Summa Theologiae* I, q. 2, art. 3).

There is a fascinating passage from Saint Thomas that very vividly makes clear how the working of the Creator can be conceptualized, how he "establishes" nature's finality for her and in her. (I thank Professor Martin Rhonheimer cordially for supplying the reference to this important text.) The passage is especially helpful inasmuch as it compares nature to art, or technology (for one can translate *ars* in this way). "Nature is distinguished from art/technology only in the fact that nature is an internal principle of causality, while art/technology is an external principle." In order to explain the "internal principle" *nature*, Thomas uses a comparison: "If the art of shipbuilding were immanent to wood, then the nature (of wood) would produce the ship, as normally happens through the art." And somewhat later in the passage Thomas clarifies once again: "Nature is nothing other than the *plan* of a certain art/technology, namely, of God's art, which is placed in things and through which the things themselves are directed toward their definite end (natura nihil est aliud quam *ratio* cuiusdam artis, scilicet divinae, indita rebus, qua ipsae res moventur ad finem determinatum)." And again Thomas illustrates this with the metaphor of shipbuilding: "It is as though the builder of a ship could impart to the pieces of wood the ability to move by themselves so as to produce the form of the ship" (*In Physic.* lib. 2, 1. 14, no. 8).

Martin Rhonheimer comments: "Nature behaves purposefully (as though she were acting intelligently and according to a plan), but since *no intelligent and intentional efficient causes can be discerned in nature herself*, this intelligent cause must be found outside of nature."

Just as the ship leads to the question, "Who built that?" so too the *manifest* experience of purposefulness, order, and beauty in nature leads to the question, "Where do these things come from?" The theory of evolution with its scientific method cannot give an answer; it can only investigate those causes at work in nature that can be identified empirically. "Therefore the theory cannot claim, either, that the theory of evolution proves that there is no designing God, whose mind is the cause of nature and of its evolution." [14]

An oft-cited remark by George G. Simpson says: "Man is the result of a purposeless and materialistic process that does not have him in mind. He was not planned." [15] If Simpson had said: With the purely quantitative-mechanical method of scientific investigation, we can identify no plan by which man originated, then his statement might have been accurate. But *this* way of observing things is not "given by nature", but rather is a willed, methodical, extremely goal-oriented option.

The deliberate restriction of one's way of observing to what is quantifiable, computable, and measurable, to material conditions and correlations, has made possible the enormous achievements of the natural sciences. But it would be extremely problematic if someone tried to declare everything that is thereby methodologically excluded from

[14] Rhonheimer, *Pro Manuscripto*, 11.
[15] George G. Simpson, *The Meaning of Evolution* (New Haven: Yale University Press, 1949), 344.

consideration to be simply nonexistent—starting with the reason and the free will that make this methodological choice possible in the first place.

It is true: the genetic code of the human being is only very slightly different from that of the chimpanzee. Yet only the human being can arrive at the idea of investigating his genetic code and that of the chimpanzee as well!

I would like to try, by means of an example, to explain what is involved in the question about the limits of the scientific method. In the August 3, 2006, issue of the German weekly news magazine *Die Zeit*, a large article appeared on the relation between "Doctor and Patient". The theme of the article: the increasingly technological character of medicine threatens to stunt the human side of the medical profession. An old problem that is once again acute. Paul Tournier, a physician from Geneva and founder of the doctors' movement Médecine de la Personne, used to say that a doctor has two hands and must use both: the one is his scientific knowledge of the human being, of the organism and its functioning. The other is his heart, his intuition, his empathy. The physician cannot do without either one if he wants to do the patient justice. Man is not a machine, even though the human body in many respects consists of complex, marvelous mechanisms and material functions. No good doctor, however, will look at man *only* as such. He will also take his soul seriously as a reality. No doctor will manage with George G. Simpson's view of man *alone*. It is false insofar as it understands itself to be a comprehensive statement about man.

And now the decisive conclusion from our comparison with the physician: *both* hands—the *scientific tools* of the doctor and the intuition he has gained from his experience, sympathy, and knowledge of human nature—*both* belong to medical *science*. Only the cooperation of *both* makes for a good doctor.

Can this model not help us to see more clearly in the debate about which we are talking here? Allow me, with all due brevity, to explain this with three examples that address the typical problem areas in the debate about evolutionism.

1. The first example is the concept of species. Darwin's famous work is entitled *The Origin of Species*. But are there such things as species in the first place? Can a purely quantitative method grasp them? Is there any place at all in evolutionary theory for them? Is not everything we call species just a momentary snapshot of the wide river of evolution? Are not concepts such as species, genera, kingdoms (the animal and plant kingdoms) just *nomina nuda*, mere words without a reality corresponding to them? On the level of what is measurable and quantifiable, *species* and *genus* are empty words. But the eyes of the mind grasp very well the fact that there is a species called "cat" (and for this the Holy Father himself, Pope Benedict, being a cat-lover, is a reliable witness!).

2. The need to rely on the "eyes of the mind" becomes even clearer when we deal with a question that today is dismissed in many quarters as "unscientific" because it is ultimately a metaphysical question lying beyond what is purely material: the question about the *substantial form*. "Whereas common sense thinks that things like trees or elephants are precisely *things*, independent beings that are more than the mere sum of their material components, the materialistic theory of evolution reduces them ... to mere epiphenomenal fluctuations of matter, which thus becomes the sole and ultimate substantial reality within the cosmos. In the final analysis, then, there would be no trees and no

elephants, but only transient aggregates of material qualities" to which we assign these names.[16]

Therefore one priority in overcoming the materialistic view of evolutionism is regaining the concept of form (as Aristoteles or Goethe understood it). The great Swiss zoologist Adolf Portmann particularly emphasized this point in his critique of Darwinism. Every living thing manifests itself as a form, as an expression of an interiority that is more than its material components. Although detailed biochemical research can methodically disregard the question about form or figure, if it is not to become blind science it cannot in the long run ignore the question of what makes a plant and a dog what they are respectively.

For all measurement and quantification presupposes that the living being—this man, this animal, this plant—exists as an independent whole that can also be grasped by the human mind.

Just as the physician must not regard the sick person as a liver, a heart, or some isolated organ, but rather as *this* human being whose heart is sick or healthy, so too the biologist who is studying a living thing will always seek to see it as a whole and to regard all its details as elements of the living whole. As Hans Urs von Balthasar put it, he will make every effort to "see the form" without which his instrumentation for measuring remains blind. "Seeing the form", however, is also the way to detect traces of the Creator.

3. That brings me to my third example. To read God's traces in creation: Is that the business of science? Scientists of former times, from Copernicus through Galileo to Newton, were convinced that it is. Besides the book of the Bible,

[16] Walker, "Schöpfung und Evolution", 59.

they are acquainted with the book of creation, in which the Creator speaks to us in legible, audible language.[17]

What a materialistic concept of science overlooks is the attitude of wonder at the "legibility" of reality. Scientific research into nature is possible only because it gives us answers. It is so "constructed" that our mind can penetrate into the laws of its construction. What could be more obvious than the hypothesis that the fact that reality can be investigated and thereby known (albeit with difficulty and only partially) is a consequence of the fact that it bears the "signature" of its Author? God speaks in the language of his creation, and our mind, which is likewise his creation, is able to hear him, listen to him, and understand him. Is that ultimately the reason why modern science developed on the native soil of the Judeo-Christian belief in creation? The oversimplified materialistic understanding of science mistakes the letters for the text. Studying and analyzing the material letters is the prerequisite for being able to read the text. But they are not the text itself; rather, they are its material conveyors. Here, too, it is evident, as in the example of the physician, that science that restricts itself *exclusively* to the material conditions is "one-handed" and thus "one-sided". It is lacking in what distinguishes man as man: his gift or talent for rising above material conditions by means of understanding and intuition and pressing onward to the meaning, the truth, the "message of the author of the text".

What practical demands result from the reflections we have just outlined? From the abundance of possible further reflections I single out only two:

[17] See R. Schaeffler, "Lesen im Buch der Welt: Ein Weg philosophischen Sprechens von Gott?" (Reading in the book of the world: a way of speaking philosophically about God?), *Stimmen der Zeit* (2006): 363–78.

1. How has "evolutionism" with its ideological materialism almost become something like a substitute religion? Why is it often defended so aggressively and emotionally? I dare say that at present there is probably no other scientific theory against which so many weighty objections exist and which is nevertheless defended by many people as completely sacrosanct. The most important objections are well known and have often been brought forward:

- the "missing links", the numerous undocumented transitional forms between the species that, after 150 years of intensive research, simply do not exist;
- the "systems-analytical" impossibility that a living system (for example, reptiles) should be rebuilt by innumerable small mutations into another living system (for example, birds);
- the problematic character of the concept of the "survival of the fittest". Marco Bersanelli has demonstrated with examples that survival is often a "matter of luck", an accident, a contingency, and not a proof of particular "fitness". The dinosaurs—and many other species—became extinct because of catastrophes and not on account of their failure to adapt.

These are only some of the most important difficulties with the theory. Why is it nevertheless so well established as a scientific theory? Because so far there is no other better theory. And because as a scientific theory it is simple and "aesthetic".

But why is it loaded down with so much ideology and made into a materialistic shibboleth? Because the alternative *world view* is the belief in creation. Anyone who says "creation" is also saying "the claim of the Creator". If there is a legible language of the Creator, then it is also something addressed to us, something that makes claims on us. One consequence thereof is an "ought", an ethical order, for instance, in the question of relations between the sexes or the defense of life. A materialistic view of evolution is easier to combine with the ambient materialism and relativism. It is no accident that ideological evolutionism was the scientific window-dressing of both Communism and National Socialism. And it still is today for economic social Darwinism, which justifies an unrestricted commercial "battle for existence".

It is delightfully illogical when Richard Dawkins, an authority on ideological Darwinism, says in an interview that he would not like to live in a Darwinian society, that it would be too inhumane.

2. There is, however, yet another reason that makes Darwinism plausible. Belief in a good Creator, in his "progetto intelligente che è il cosmo" (intelligent design that is the cosmos) (Pope Benedict XVI, General audience of November 9, 2005), is called into question by almost endless cruelties: Why this laborious way of evolution, with its countless attempts, dead ends, with its billions of years of time and its expanding universe; the gigantic explosions of supernovae, the simmering of the elements in the nuclear fusion of the stars, the bone-grinding mechanism of evolution with its endless fresh starts and exterminations, its catastrophes and cruelties, down to the incomprehensible brutalities of life and survival? Does it not make more sense to see the whole thing as the blind play of accidents in a nature devoid of plan? Is that not more honest than the attempts of Leibniz, for instance, at theodicy, which end up in a quandary for lack of arguments? Is it not more plausible simply to say: Yes, the world is indeed that cruel.

One thing should be noted at the conclusion of our reflections: In our apologetics we should not be over-hasty about trying to point out "intelligent design" everywhere. Like Job, we do not know the answer to suffering. We have only received one answer. God himself gave it. The Logos, through whom and in whom everything was created, took on flesh and, with it, the whole history of the universe, of evolution, with its grandiose and its gruesome aspects. He took upon himself the whole negative burden of suffering, destruction, and, above all, moral evil. *The Cross* is the key to God's plan and counsel. As important and as indispensable a renewed, in-depth effort in matters of *natural philosophy* is, the message of the Cross is God's ultimate wisdom. For through his holy Cross he reconciled the whole world. Yet the Cross is the gate leading to resurrection.

In his first Easter homily, Pope Benedict said:

> Christ's Resurrection . . . , if we may borrow the language of the theory of evolution, . . . is the greatest "mutation", absolutely the most crucial leap into a totally new dimension that there has ever been in the long history of life and its development: a leap into a completely new order that does concern us, and concerns the whole of history. . . . It is a qualitative leap in the history of "evolution" and of life in general toward a new future life, toward a new world, which, starting from Christ, already continuously permeates this world of ours, transforms it, and draws it to itself. (Homily at the Easter Vigil, April 15, 2006)

If the Resurrection of Christ is, so to speak "the greatest mutation", or as Pope Benedict says in the same homily, "an explosion of love that dissolved the hitherto indissoluble compenetration of 'dying and becoming'", then we may also say: Here is the destination "of evolution". Seen from its conclusion and accomplishment, its meaning also becomes manifest. Although in its individual steps it may seem aimless and without direction, the long way did have a meaning when viewed from the perspective of Easter. It is not that "the way is the goal"; rather, the Resurrection is the meaning of the way.

DISCUSSION

The discussion recorded here followed the lectures that were presented to the Schülerkreis *on September 1 and repeated on September 2 in the presence of Pope Benedict XVI. The subheadings note which lecture served as the basis for each part of the discussion.*

September 1, Morning

Lecture by Peter Schuster:
"Evolution and Design" (see pages 27–60)

Theo Schafer: Both of my questions concern chance. First, has the concept of "chance" been sufficiently well defined in biology and the natural sciences? And second, can a distinction be made between subjective and objective chance?

Vincent Twomey: In your second point you talk about probability and chance. Don't scientists nowadays avoid the term "necessity" and speak only about probability?

Ludwig Weimer: Is evolution a simple, gradual path that can be explained, or were there also inexplicable leaps? How, for example, did primordial cells manage to undertake a division of labor, specialization, and cooperation? Did this lead immediately to the eukaryotes in a two-stage process, or were there many wrong turns and misfires in between?

Peter Schuster: I would like to begin with the last question. The difference between eukaryotes and prokaryotes does not fall within my field of specialization; nevertheless, I think that I can say something about it: There are several ideas about the development of the eukaryotes through endosymbiosis. What is certain is that over a long period of time there was a global environmental change in the earth's atmosphere that was connected with the fact that free oxygen became a component of the air. Oxygen is absolutely poisonous for all the organisms that populated the earth before this phase (basically, various forms of bacteria), as it is for our cells, too. It would destroy our cells, but evidently a species of bacteria developed that was able to deal with oxygen, and that species made its way into our cells in the form of our mitochondria. This was one of the most important prerequisites for living organisms: if they are exposed to free atmospheric oxygen, they must also be capable of dealing with it.

The endosymbionts hypothesis [that is, that a cell can thrive in symbiosis with a smaller bacterium that it has internalized] has already been very strongly corroborated. There is one finding that for me is convincing: the mitochondria in our cells possess not only their own, but also an additional second membrane. This double membrane comes about when cells that already have a membrane enter into a host and become wrapped in its cell membrane as well. Indeed, the mitochondria that carry on the oxygen exchange in our cells have these two membranes. Whereas the earlier anaerobic organisms could not survive in the oxygenated atmosphere, the endosymbionts could. Besides that, there was another effect that was essential for further development: it became possible to change metabolism completely. In mitochondria, oxidation processes occur that produce considerably more energy than the fermentation processes previously conducted by the prokaryotes. In other words, during this phase, for those organisms that had mitochondria, energy became "cheap". And so oxygen was at first an environmental poison; then came the possibility to make use of it metabolically; and finally it became a source that made drastically higher levels of energy available.

It appears that this endosymbiosis occurred several times. Plants, too, have incorporated a second organism, the so-called chloroplasts, the forerunners of which likewise existed in nature previously and which are responsible for photosynthesis. As we said, at the moment the most probable hypothesis for the development of eukaryotes is this coming together and working together by way of division of labor.

As for the questions concerning chance, I will start with necessity as described by Jacques Monod in his book *Chance and Necessity*. We speak about necessity when from a given state another unambiguously defined state follows unavoidably. There are such definite sequential processes in nature, but in biology they are rather uncommon, since typical events occur not inevitably but only with particular degrees of probability. Probability, we can say, is the mathematical sister of chance. It is easy and at the same time difficult to define chance. The chemical processes that go on in biology are coordinated in enormous networks. Starting from one point in the network there are a large number of parallel processes, for example, those that lead to correct copies and to bad copies or mutations. Now where does chance come from, since all these reactions follow a certain mechanism that can be understood and analyzed? This is true for correct replication just as it is for a mutation. These mechanisms have also been investigated very precisely by means of examples. Now chance comes in by way of probability. Let us assume that we had one thousand possible reactions, which of course are not all equally likely, but for the sake of simplicity we will suppose that they have equal probability. The physicist Ludwig Boltzmann of Vienna has shown what kind of statistics should be used for events in the atomic and molecular realm. Among other things, his results show that the average deviation in the number of particles for N particles amounts to $\pm\sqrt{N}$ (plus or minus the square root of N). For our example with 1,000 parallel reaction pathways, that means that over the course of 1,000 individual reactions we will find in each pathway 1 ± 1 particle(s), most often 0, 1, or 2. We will say, then, that the occurrence of a particular reaction is a chance event, something determined by chance. But let us assume that we had 10^{23} particles, which is the equivalent of the number of water molecules in 3 grams of water; then we would observe $10^{20} \pm 10^{10}$ molecules on each pathway. The statistical variations would not be measurable, and so in fact we would measure the same number of particles on all the pathways. For typical events in chemistry, the situation with the high number of particles holds true, but for biology, especially for the biology of reproduction and heredity, the first-mentioned example with the small number of particles applies. Mendel's laws of heredity, therefore, are only statistically true, that is, when a sufficiently large number of individual observations are being considered.

This sort of chance has a component of incomplete information. We could formulate this in another way: If we had complete information about all the details of the ongoing processes (which for practical reasons we could never obtain), then our statistical uncertainty would be much, much smaller, perhaps even in the vicinity of zero, and the occurrence of events would be predictable.

But other additional difficulties arise. In the first place, the individual reaction pathways are traveled with different frequencies. As a result, the most common pathways, those with the highest probabilities, can be selected, and in contrast the products from the uncommon pathways appear to occur by chance. This state of affairs is found in nature with the frequencies of correct copies and mutations. The frequency of all mutations taken together is very small, and furthermore there are a very large number of possible mutations. The probability of the occurrence of a particular mutation becomes so small that we speak of chance.

In biology a further element to be considered is the self-reinforcement of the copying processes. Through copying processes a single molecule can be replicated practically without limit, from one original to ten thousand or more. The numbers of carriers of an advantageous mutation will increase—even if its initial probability was very small. But which one of many equally valuable mutations will be selected is the point where chance comes in. It is not a question of completely random phenomena, as we find with dice, where all possibilities really have equal value. Yet the fact that I can indeed make a selection only once produces a situation that is similar to a throw of the dice. Chance is a consequence of the low probabilities that we have for these processes and the fact that we can perceive them through their self-reinforcing activity. If there were no self-reinforcement, a low probability would mean that we could never observe the rare processes. But as it is, an event with low probability manifests itself exclusively in the unpredictability of the specific advantageous variants that are selected.

Theo Schafer: Can we understand the answer that you are giving to mean that in biology and quantum mechanics, for example, the reasons for processes can be stated, but not their *telos* [end or purpose]?

Peter Schuster: The search for a *telos*, in the sense of final cause, is not immediately the task of research in the natural sciences. *Telos* does play a role, however, in the question of whether or not observations require a *telos* to "explain" them, as the natural sciences understand explanation. In my answer I did not touch on this question; rather, I addressed exclusively the problem of *predictability*. The greater the share of chance in an event, the less its occurrence can be predicted reliably.

Quantum mechanics introduces yet another form of chance, *genuine* or fundamental chance, into the biological event. Quantum mechanics currently teaches that there is such a thing as genuine chance, beyond which we cannot inquire. Before we merely used to say that for *practical* reasons we could not predict what event would occur, since we could not retrace all the individual steps of the wide variety of molecules involved. Yet even if all the complex processes were to be broken down into the individual reactions, the uncertainty at the level of quantum mechanics would still remain. Therefore with biological processes, too, when I treat them (as any chemist does) as chemical reactions whose basis is ultimately quantum mechanics, I would run into quantum phenomena, even though I began with an empirical description that at first knows nothing about quantum-theoretical uncertainty. Fundamental chance is added to the chance stemming from practical reasons. When we strive for ever-greater atomic analysis, sooner or later we always end up at the quantum-mechanical problem of the indescribability of certain phenomena.

Robert Spaemann: Should we not perhaps say that chance is a reflexive concept? For basically it negates something. Suppose, for example, that I see a reddish-pink object up ahead and then three or four meters farther on a similar pink. Now if someone asks how that happens, you would not answer that it is chance, but rather, as Karl Valentin once said, it's "nothin' at all". That means that the endless instances of interference among causal processes interests us only when something results from it that looks like an intention. Someone who then believes that there is nevertheless no intention will use the word "chance".

Assuming the case that we find on a park bench two cigarette butts, a beer bottle, and a couple of bricks, we would say: that is nothing at all. But if we found the same assortment of objects on five benches, we would say: that is chance (whereby it then becomes increasingly less probable that it is really chance).

Chance simply means: there is nothing behind it; it is a matter of an interference that only looks as though it were meaningful. Would you agree with that?

Peter Schuster: I agree with that completely and would just like to add one small detail: the relation of a mutation to its selection is very often described as accidental only because it is uncorrelated. The fact that a particular mutation takes place has no influence on the selection process. And this lack of correlation led in this case to the concept of chance.

You proposed the example with the park bench and the bricks. I like to put it even more dramatically: It is quite causal that a roofer takes his break at a particular time and while doing so does not notice that a brick rolls off the roof. He takes his break every day at this moment in time. Every day also, between eight and ten o'clock, a person walks in a particular direction past the house. That, too, is causal, because the person is going to work or to buy something. But then one time a temporal coincidence occurs, and the person is struck by the brick. It was uncorrelated, and we would say: *by chance* the person was walking by at that precise moment, and so the dramatic event happened.

Christoph Cardinal Schonborn: I have seldom heard it said with such clarity that evolutionary biology has parted ways with the small steps of the Darwinian theory. What, then, are the large steps like? I would like to combine this question with a crux of contemporary biology, namely, the concept of species. Do these steps have something to do with the emergence of species? Darwin titled his book *The Origin of Species*. So the question arises: Do species exist in the first place, and do scientists today see an intrinsic connection between the steps and the species?

Antoine Saroyan: Does biology have an answer to the question of why the "leaps" or mutations occur, or are these accepted as a given and then reproduced experimentally?

Vincent Twomey: How does one get from something simple to something more complicated? Is there some sort of preprogramming already included in it?

Peter Schuster: First I will address the subject of the small steps. Darwin insisted on the small steps, and in the nineteenth century all biologists who studied natural selection would have agreed with him. The consensus then was that these small steps had manifested themselves in a continuous development. There are cases in which a continuous development does in fact take place at a more or less constant speed, but there are at least as many or more cases in which this is not so. There is no biological or molecular-biological reason for the fact that Darwin insisted on small steps; rather, the reason for it is historical. The selection biologists of that time were convinced that one can produce any form of organism, fine-tuned at will in all its characteristics.

Mutation is per se a discrete step. At a particular place along the string of genetic information one can have either an A or a U (or else a T, depending on whether the molecule is DNA or RNA). Therefore if an A is replaced by a G, a C, or a T, we are dealing with discrete steps, which have consequences that allow for no intermediate possibilities. No continuum can be produced by individual mutations. The question of whether there can be a quasi-continuous development ultimately boils down to the question of whether all these mutations can result in characteristics that are so close together that they manifest only very small differences. The answer is: No. There are certain intermediate stages that we cannot reach with mutations, and therefore there will inevitably be big steps as well. Therefore it is wrong to insist exclusively on small steps.

Today we know that only certain phenotypes exist, without transitional forms in between. There are only certain forms that can be realized. The question for evolutionary biology today is: What are these forms, and where, on the other hand, are there continuous transitions (for instance, in the measurements of a full-grown individual)? For example, in a population there can be individuals of every size, whereas in other areas, for instance, with regard to organs, only discrete steps are possible.

As for the question about the concept of species: The concept of species is probably the only higher concept in biology that we can call well defined: Individuals of different species cannot have fertile offspring. Over the spectrum of biology there are a few anomalies, but they do no damage to the definition of species. Basically, what is presumably the most important path to the formation of species has already been correctly described in synthetic biology. First, a geographical division of a population into sub-populations comes about. Through this separation the sub-populations develop in distinctive ways and go in different directions (for example, through a different sequence of mutations, a different environment, and different adaptations). And so this results in a diminished fertility between the different sub-populations.

At this point we come to the definition of race or breed, which of course is often used incorrectly. For example, within the human population, there are strictly speaking no "races", which are, after all, defined by the fact that members of different races, while capable of reproducing, have a lower fertility rate than do individuals within a race. If we imagine, now, that the development of the races continues independently, then the formation of species begins, and isolation results. The donkey and the horse are the best example that we have: they still have offspring, the mule and the hinny, both of which, however, are sterile. In the next step, a process of adaptation takes place. For if unfruitful offspring are generated, it is a waste of energy for individuals of different races to keep copulating with each other. Then it becomes advantageous if an additional isolation comes about, which can be governed, for instance, by chemistry, by the various sorts of pheromones, or even by physiology. This, briefly summarized, is the process of species formation according to the synthetic theory. Today we know that there are also other types of species formation for which geographical isolation is not necessary. But basically this, too, was already recognized during the development of the synthetic theory.

It becomes difficult with the terms for the superior divisions that are derived from morphology, for instance, the feline or canine predators, which we distinguish from one another by their morphology but which no longer have these distinctive features. Here comparative DNA-sequencing has been of help. We see that these superior structures in the biosphere are connected to certain points in the ramification of the phylogenetic tree. Although there are very many forms, one can distinguish cats and dogs by their respective phylogenetic trees. The trees are very close to each other, however, which is why even morphologists have difficulties with this distinction and cannot always work with 100 percent accuracy.

Christoph Cardinal Schonborn: Clearly, therefore, the leaps and the species are not the same thing. For me the question still remains: *Why* these leaps? And the old question that I have very often read in the related literature: Has the existence of transitional forms between species been proved according to scientific norms [*lege artis*]? *The Origin of Species*—one species derived from an earlier one: What does that look like in relation to the leaps, and is there really any proof of evolutionary steps from one species to another, not just theoretically, but factually?

Peter Schuster: There are observations concerning correlation with the environment in the formation of races, for instance in the case of English butterflies [or gypsy moths] that changed their color in response to environmental pollution. Among salamanders and amphibians, there is one example in which currently reproductive isolation has almost been reached.

One very persuasive finding, in my opinion, is also a historical one: the phylogenetic tree. It can be traced and reconstructed at the molecular level by comparing large areas of the genome. Transitional forms of the most varied sorts have been found. Development "by leaps and bounds" has to be seen, first and foremost, in the fact that we are dealing with processes on different time scales. On the one hand, there is a short time scale, in which very much changes, and, on the other hand, a long time scale also in which little changes. If both processes, the slow and the fast, are charted on one time scale, then it looks like a step or a leap. Much if not everything that has been discovered by paleobiology speaks in favor of these sorts of processes. Naturally they cannot be unbroken, since a mutation is always a leap. The real question is whether the mutation manifests itself in something that is infinitesimally small or in a step. The leaps that we see in experiments and computer simulations have only one thing in common with species formation: the fact that they are adaptation processes. Species formation, by the current definition, is limited to sexual populations, because otherwise one could not use the reproduction argument. Among bacteria, too, of course, there are degrees of affinity that are demonstrable at the molecular level, but in that case there are other mechanisms that have nothing to do with sexual isolation. The leaps that I have shown today in my illustrations concern asexual populations, namely, bacteria and molecules in a test tube. The effects of mutations in diploid sets of chromosomes are similar to the results in haploid organisms. In the latter, however, because of recombination, there is a larger repertoire of variants than is found in bacteria.

Christoph Cardinal Schonborn: The historical proof cannot be confirmed experimentally. If I am looking at it correctly, the genetic relatedness of all living things is something that we are overwhelmingly more conscious of thanks to genetic research, but that really does not answer the question about the "family tree". The building blocks of life are the same from the very beginning; the letters are without exception the same. Therefore we are really related with every living thing. But these building blocks alone do not yet add up to what we observe in the things that are alive: life in its great diversity. Darwin's claim to have explained "the origin of species" has not yet been made good in this respect.

Peter Schuster: I would like to express myself a little more clearly. There are two possible ways of looking at history that are completely independent of each other. The one is paleontology or paleobiology. Basically, in the middle of the last century this was the only available possibility. In this discipline, conclusions about family trees were drawn from morphological similarities, for instance, from skeletal structures preserved in fossils. Then in the mid-1960s another independent way of investigating the past developed. If two species have a common ancestor, then through a sequence of mutations (running through the two distinct lines of descent down to the present) they must exhibit differences from that ancestor that have a historical component. For there is a historical series of mutations for each of the two lines. At first the number of sequences available was very limited. The real breakthrough was achieved in the 1970s, when DNA-sequencing became simple and inexpensive as a result of new techniques. Now we have a great abundance of sequences that we can compare. We have, so to speak, not only models but also opportunities to test these against a wide variety of examples.

The thing that fascinates me is that when this genealogical tree is reconstructed from the molecular data, and thus when scientists ascertain the family relations through the history of the mutations that have occurred, the results are the same as those from paleobiology. It is also fascinating that in molecular biology there is something like a molecular clock. The number of mutations annually (as evidence among vertebrates interestingly suggests) seems to be a constant. Since I can now reconstruct the mutations from several paleobiological findings, I can calibrate the clock. The results agree essentially with the geological dating. Of course there are certain anomalies, and even the constant for the number of mutations annually is only a rough approximation, because there are various causes for mutations, many of which also are connected with the length of a generation. But it is remarkable that with vertebrates we can determine the time scale along with the reconstruction of the genealogical tree.

With invertebrate animals there are still problems. Here the correlation with the dating of the ramifications of the genealogical tree did not go so well. Today we know that in invertebrate animals the "clocks" are not synchronized. The existence of a molecular-biological clock for the reconstruction of the past, therefore, applies only to vertebrates, and to that extent it does not hold true for other organisms. Admittedly, a temporal reconstruction is subject to error, but this has nothing to do with the structure of these trees. One of the most convincing arguments for me is that morphology, on the one hand, and the affinities determined by DNA, on the other hand, lead to the same result.

A few interesting things: Earlier, when scientists were studying the genome of bacteria, it was discovered that bacteria actively exchange information with each other. Because of this "horizontal" transfer of genes, the phylogenetic tree in the early phase of biological evolution becomes a complicated structure, because the genes from one organism are transferred to another. We experience horizontal gene transfer in our time, too, for instance, when bacteria exchange among themselves information about our pharmaceutical achievements. Especially in hospitals, where many antibiotics are used, the result is a large-scale exchange of resistance factors. This exchange essentially stops, however, in the eukaryotes, or else it occurs only very seldom. Otherwise we would not be able to reconstruct genealogical trees.

Siegfried Wiedenhofer: You have shown that a molecular-biological theory of evolution no longer assumes that evolution is a constant, necessary process of optimization. My first question is: What does that mean, precisely? Is it true in every respect, in the short term, the middle term, and the long term? And my second question: Does this also mean that another "fundamental dogma" of biology is being called into question, namely, the doctrine that every organism tries to propagate its genes and that evolution is therefore a "competitive undertaking"?

Paul Erbrich: It is utterly amazing how well scientists can simulate a Darwinian evolution process with molecular systems and how it also demonstrates that this mechanism is evidently a real mechanism. The problem, in my opinion, arises when we go from the simulation models to real organisms. Let us take as an example the evolutionary step that occurred with the emergence of oxygen. Since oxygen is strong poison to a cell, the living things in an oxygenated environment have to develop enzymes that immediately destroy the radicals containing oxygen that can be produced when oxygen makes its way into the cell interior. The matter becomes even more complicated when, in addition to that, they "want" to use oxygen as an electron acceptor so as to obtain "cheap" energy. For that, they need dozens of enzymes that, on account of their dependence on one another, all have to become capable of functioning at the same time, certainly not with the perfection they have today, but still to the extent that they can compete with the anaerobic bacteria that were successful until then. Here the question arises whether such a development can come about solely through Darwin's mechanism of chance (random exchange of bases, random recombination, random duplication of genes) with subsequent selection of the better adapted.

Peter Schuster: In answer to the question about molecular-biological optimization: There are two points involved in my statement about optimization. First, several processes are taking place on the same time scale, during which the world has already changed again, while optimization is adapting. In such a dynamic, the actual development is never optimal. We are acquainted with this phenomenon from various other fields as well. In natural biological development, co-evolution takes place in every ecosystem: when one species adapts to another species, then the latter has meanwhile already gone through a development again. For example, if a frog has developed a sticky tongue in order to catch flies more easily, then the flies are not going to remain at the same level, either, but rather develop a secretion that breaks down that substance so that they can go free again. That is one example of a dynamic process driven by competition among species in an ecosystem. Mutual adaptation prevents them from attaining an optimum.

The second point concerns the number of possibilities from among which an optimum is sought. With a single protein, such an optimization is quite possible—both in nature and in a laboratory experiment. But now the units become larger. In a complete organism there are, as I showed you at the start, an immense number of possibilities for various sequences, for mutual gradation, for regulation. Nature then develops further in such a way that it develops functioning units and transforms and further alters them, but no longer optimizes them. This also has to do with the fact that we are dealing with a historical process that we can no longer retrace, because there have been too many steps in between. Thus, for instance, with respect to the number of limbs, the decision among the vertebrates was made some time between the fish and the amphibians. When we look today at how laboriously birds work with a beak, we would probably allot them two more limbs. The same is true, for example, at cocktail parties, when you would like to distribute your calling cards and at the same time have to hold a glass. Here, too, another pair of hands would be an advantage. What I am trying to say is that the more complicated the units become, the higher we have gone in our development, the more difficult optimization becomes. Ultimately we are dealing with an array of functioning organisms, because those that were incapable of functioning have disappeared. Adaptation, therefore, can take place only within the framework of what is presently available and possible. Really thoroughgoing variation, in order to reach an optimum, is no longer possible.

September 1, Afternoon

Lecture by Robert Spaemann:
"Common Descent and Intelligent Design"
(see pages 61–69)

Christoph Cardinal Schonborn: Thank you, Professor Spaemann, for this marvelous, beautiful supplement. We are now confronted with a very clear complementarity, and I think that we should deliberate on it in our discussion.

Not long ago I had to give a lecture in Rimini on the subject of creation and evolution, and I tried to illustrate this complementarity with an example that to me seems helpful. The late Swiss physician Paul Tournier, who founded a movement of doctors called Médecine de la Personne, always used to say: A doctor has two hands. He must have a really good command of the natural sciences. But he also needs another hand in order to be a good doctor: empathy, intuition, the holistic view. Ultimately he does not have to deal with a liver or a heart, but rather with a *human being* who has a liver disease or coronary problems. Only when he uses both hands together is he a good doctor. I think that we must always pose the reflexive question about the subject within the natural sciences as well.

This morning we got a glimpse of the fascinating achievements of the biosciences, yet all that cannot be found among the chimpanzees, even though they possess a genome that is 99 percent the same as ours, but only among human beings. Only man pursues science. The reflection on what it means to be able to pursue science is the prerequisite for the existence of science. For if this "step back" were not taken, there would be no scientific theory, either. Alfred North Whitehead once said: "Scientists animated by the purpose of proving that they are purposeless constitute an interesting subject for study." There is hardly any activity more goal-oriented than experimental science, which with fascinating cleverness develops methods of finding out nature. What I miss in the discussion of evolution is the reflection on the one who is investigating evolution. As Egon Friedell once said ironically, "And then man became capable of evolutionary theory, after a long history of evolution." This should give us food for thought, because it cannot be explained solely by material prerequisites for development. It also pertains to some extent to what Professor Spaemann has said. I would go another step farther and say that this is the case not only between the natural sciences and the humanities, but also within the natural sciences themselves: They are an extremely human project that is possible only for beings endowed with subjectivity. But they have evidently ruled out thinking about the subject that is undertaking this exclusion. Of course, great natural scientists again and again have taken this "step back" and reflected on their presuppositions. The presupposition, as Professor Spaemann, too, has said, is that nature is legible, that it is written in an intelligible language, that the book of creation can be decoded. As Thomas Aquinas said: *Res inter duos intellectus constituta.* A thing is established between two reasons, namely, divine reason that has devised it and human reason that can fathom it.

Robert Spaemann: Concerning the legible aspect, there is a saying by Michel Foucault: "We must not imagine that the world turns a legible face toward us." Foucault rejected everything that was based on legibility. For example, he considered even discourse to be sheer power brokering. A common effort to reach the truth cannot exist at all, because it leads to nothing. The world shows us no legible face. That would be the other way of looking at it.

But when you say that it is a question of a discrepancy in science itself, and that science must reflect on it, I am not quite sure whether I can agree. After all, there are excellent scientists who do not initiate such a reflection at all, or at least not *as* scientists. The question is whether this reflection must be taken up by science as such. Presumably it does not have to be, even though a scientist who brackets it off runs the risk of overestimating the capacity of his own science. But this is a psychological aspect that pertains to the scientist. From a purely methodological perspective, I am not sure that it has to be.

Christoph Cardinal Schonborn: Allow me to clarify here. He does not have to within the methodology of his work, which of course consists in bracketing off these *meta*-physical questions. Indeed, that is precisely what is responsible for the successful history of the method in question. Yet it is overstepping a boundary when the natural scientist denies, for instance, his subjectivity (which makes it possible for him to pursue science in the first place) along with the concomitant metaphysical reality.

Ludwig Weimer: I was struck by a slight tension between two passages in your text, which perhaps a theologian would notice more readily than a philosopher. It concerns the *possibility* of God revealing himself in creation, which is to say the *legibility* of the world, in a stronger theological sense.

On the one hand, you say that only "by a distant analogy" can I put myself in the place of a bat that is hungry. Later you say that all of creation, including man, "is founded upon the same will of a Divine Wisdom" (and therefore is more than merely analogous), and that God wills that we discover him as the Creator of life and thank him. This is expressed with great refinement and caution. I need only to thank him and to discover him as the ultimate origin. But how do I get to know him more closely? Here I am not thinking about events in salvation history, which God likewise makes known to us only in an analogous manner, but rather about God's speech in the natural order.

Here I notice a little tension. The creature is supposed to discover its Creator as its origin; this means that there is, therefore, a divine wisdom that must be built in so that it can find this God. But if God were to manifest himself as world, then we would be worshipping a bit of the world, an idol. God must be invisible to us, so that we do not mistake him for a bit of the world. The less he manifests himself in a material way, the more we recognize that he stands opposite the world as its Creator. Is it not true after all, then, that a human being—perhaps at first through the history of religion or mythology, and later by enlightened faith—must acquire the ability to put himself mentally in the place of this *other*? Since God is something so different from man, how could he reveal himself as the *Creator* (who is not only man's interiority or a pantheistic "It"), if man could not imagine himself in his place at all? Here I see a certain tension: Are you referring to a permanent split in our world view, or did you mean this statement about "the same will" only in an analogous sense?

Robert Spaemann: Basically the world is transparent to the one who has left his footprints in it. But human beings are inclined to ignore these footprints. Although you say that God does not manifest himself visibly in the world, I think that he does too show himself. In the Christian faith, the director himself appears in the film. Dum visibiliter Deum cognoscimus, per hunc in invisibilem amorem rapiamur (While we recognize God in visible form, let us be snatched up by him into an invisible love). In this respect, God does manifest himself; this, however, is not a matter of philosophy but rather a matter of the Christian faith. The reason for it, however, is the weakness of man, whose capacity to see God has been darkened by sin. Therefore, as Augustine says, God himself appears as a bit of the world.

Udo Schiffers: I would like to refer to Professor Schuster's lecture. The lecture helped me to overcome the final temptation as well, which is to try to introduce God by way of explaining some gap or other. There is, however, if I have understood Professor Spaemann correctly, a parallel level, a meta-level, where faith decisions come into play very early on and where some are convinced by a philosophy of chance, and others of the existence of a Creator God, which in either case goes beyond the methodology of technical science.

I like to see philosophy—as Professor Spaemann does—in its critical function as an *ars quaerendi* [art of seeking]. It is the intellectual place where, starting from faith and knowledge, we can attempt a holistic concept of "world view".

In this connection I would like to ask a question: As far as I know, Teilhard de Chardin reflected very profoundly on the subject of cognition and tried to work it into an evolutionary view of reality through the concept of the noosphere, a sort of collective spirit. To what extent is that still a part of reflections today? Is it not legitimate to incorporate such a concept as well? Putting it another way, to what extent is someone like Ken Wilbur taken seriously? He, too, attempts to work the subject's ability to know and understand the world into a comprehensive world view.

Peter Schuster: A preliminary comment: I have already been criticized today for having used the word "beautiful", which is actually none of my business. The natural scientist is supposed to swear off colloquial speech entirely, and that causes difficulties. We cannot help making use of anthropomorphic terms everywhere, and then we explain at length, usually in the footnotes, that fundamentally we do not mean them in that way; we just have no other way of speaking.

I would be glad to elaborate on your comment, which is very reassuring to me in terms of my world view. Something that has bothered me the whole time is that people look for gaps in the science so as to hide in them subjective things that are inaccessible to natural science. This starts with the argument that free will originates in Heisenberg's uncertainty principle. You put it quite well: It cannot be God's fate to be interpreted into all these gaps and to be constricted by further scientific findings.

This morning a question was asked about complex behavior resulting from simple rules. There is a very fine study, done quite a while ago, in which Stephen Wolfram observed a classification among much simpler things than the ones I showed you. The simple rules that then produce patterns essentially result in two types of behavior. In the one type, they arrive after a rather long time at a completely ordered state. In the other type, they exhibit chaotic behavior. Finally, there is another very small group of such cellular automatons that is interesting inasmuch as they display neither the one nor the other type of behavior. It was possible to show that these automatons can be used as calculators. They have an intrinsic structure that gives them great possibilities. Our life processes seem to lie, similarly, between complete order and chaos, which is often expressed in the phrase "life at the edge of chaos".

When I speak with my colleagues from the field of physics, they say that they can imagine many universes, but there is only a very narrow range that is in keeping with the actual development. This depends, for example, on the charges [of subatomic particles] that come to be in the particular universe. Likewise there is a relative narrow range that leads to those terrestrial conditions that were responsible for developments, some of which we postulate and some of which we can see through the fossil record. The framework within which our laws of nature stand and within which a biological development is possible is only a narrow corridor. If I were a theologian, I would try to see precisely in this the working of a Creator, not in some areas that are not yet understood.

Werner Neuer: Professor Schuster, at the beginning of your lecture you emphasized that you are making an attempt to trace all biological processes back to chemical and physical events. I consider this a perfectly legitimate working hypothesis, at least with the qualification that this should not lead to any sort of prohibitions on thought. Even in biology, in my opinion, there should be an openness to the concept of teleology. In Germany the American intelligent design movement is not highly regarded, because it is often mistaken for creationism. Here, though, a clear distinction should be made. In the intelligent design movement, there are renowned scientists, who for example have introduced the concept of irreducible complexity, which means that in the world there are living systems that cannot be derived solely from physical processes. We should be able to discuss this openly. In fact, in astronomy, too, there is a project in which scientists are trying to find extraterrestrial intelligence. This project presupposes that information that can be decoded is recognizable in principle. I would also advocate admitting the legitimacy of the question about teleology as a scientific question as well.

Peter Schuster: In answer to the first question: What I mean when I say that biological processes can be traced back to chemistry and physics is often misunderstood. I myself come from a time in which the physicists claimed that chemistry was basically nothing other than physics. In principle the physicists proved to be right, but because chemistry uses concepts that physics as such knew nothing about, it continued. Among these, for example, is the chemical concept of substance. Also the ways in which chemical reactions occur, for instance, are proper to chemistry. And if people today say that the program of molecular biology is to succeed in reducing biological processes to chemistry and physics, this naturally does not mean that there is no independent element in biology that would more than justify it, both methodologically and with respect to its contents. Such concepts are, for example, the concept of the information that is used in the reproduction of organisms, the concept of the complexity of networks of reaction processes, to a degree unknown either in physics or chemistry, or the concept of *autopoiesis* for a cell that displays certain kinds of stability, even when almost all its molecules have been exchanged. These are dynamic structures, the chemical and physical components of which are replaced on an ongoing basis. There

133

are molecules that are renewed after only fifteen minutes, while long-living molecules are found especially in the brain. Self-maintenance is a unique feature of biology.

The reductionist program does not want to explain biology in terms of physics exclusively, but it does want to show that the processes that occur in biology can be explained on the basis of other sciences. Natural scientists understand "explain" to mean something very simple: that one can reduce a certain state of affairs to a simpler conceptual system, and to some extent one can in fact trace complex processes in biology back to simpler, chemical processes. Therefore I myself quite deliberately do not use the word "reductionism", but rather "reductionist work program".

Another comment on Professor Spaemann's double coding, which I find quite fascinating: It was in fact one and the same person who introduced both codes. And therefore, in my opinion, the one message is as good as the other: the music is as good as the text. That is not a case for Occam's razor. In nature, too, such multiple applications occur, for example, when the same bit of DNA in a virus or a bacterium encodes two different proteins. The second coding in this case is a great discovery. It has nothing to do with Occam's razor, which in this context would exclude one of two parts having equal value.

Siegfried Wiedenhofer: Professor Spaemann, the unity of reality is a central category for the discussion between philosophy and the natural sciences. If one assumes at the outset, as you have done, an insurmountable dualism in our ways of knowing (a knowledge of material functional correlations, on the one hand, and the knowledge of meaning, on the other hand), then the problem of unity and of the possibility for dialogue arises. You have—at least indirectly—mentioned the possibility of regarding those material functional correlations as the necessary conditions for human life, so that a hierarchical understanding of reality becomes visible in the background. Then the question arises to what extent science helps philosophy and theology to recognize meaning.

Actually, with the idea of creation you have suggested a *theological* solution after all, which surprised me. Only in the idea of creation can the unity of science be substantiated. My question is now: Is a philosophical substantiation not still necessary, at least in the sense that the experience of not knowing reality as a whole is always a premise of our scientific knowledge, and of our religious knowledge also, but in another manner? And would this experience of the limitations of each approach not itself be a point of departure for a dialogue?

Robert Spaemann: I meant to say that only with the idea of a Creator (which, by the way, is not only a religious idea but also a philosophical one; after all, Whitehead is a mathematician and philosopher, not a theologian) do we conceptualize a convergence of the processes that ultimately lead to the outcome of human life, which is characterized by the emancipation from the conditions of its origin. You spoke about meaning that is irreducible. Instead, I would speak first about the subject. I would have liked to hear Professor Schuster's opinion about this, too. Biologists speak about complexity. But what we experience first of all is something quite *simple*, for example, "I", a feeling or an urge. An urge that is experienced is not something complex at all, no more than a subject that thinks of itself when it says "I". Complexity, our experience tells us, is a condition that makes it possible for these things to emerge. Yet what emerges is obviously something else entirely. This "something else entirely" then becomes the acting subject of science, too. The subject that pursues science is, therefore, something entirely other than what is discovered in science.

As for theology, it does not need knowledge from the natural sciences in principle but rather for a pragmatic reason: because it has to know what human beings know at the moment when this knowledge steps forward with the claim to have understood the thing itself, whereas only the conditions have been understood. At this juncture, nonetheless, theology has to be informed about the scientific findings. But viewed thematically, it is not necessary for theology itself to see these correlations. Otherwise, logically, there would have been no valid theology until there was a valid natural science, which was plainly not the case.

Peter Schuster: I would like to comment on the question of whether complexity in biology is perhaps only a consequence of the scientific description of biological phenomena. From the scientist's perspective, a phenomenon is perceived as complex when the predictions that I would like to make about further behavior become very difficult for any reason at all. In this sense one could describe the weather, for instance, as complex, because it is difficult to analyze it in all its details. In fact it is very difficult for the physicist to model the dynamics of the earth's atmosphere. Although the individual processes are simple, I have here a genuine phenomenon of complexity. The atmosphere, therefore, is *seemingly* simple, because we understand well the physical laws behind it, but the dynamics that result from them make predictions very difficult. This is precisely what we have now in biology, on a large scale and on quite different levels. Complexity, therefore, is not just an attempt—perhaps a clumsy one—at describing a phenomenon, but rather it is an inherent component of these phenomena.

On the other hand, the description of complexity within the framework of natural science is very new. It is often typical of such recent developments that concepts change, and no suitable way of characterizing a phenomenon has yet been found. Today research institutes that study complexity are springing up everywhere, and this, in my opinion, will lead to a clearer definition of the problems.

Robert Spaemann: We can never observe simplicity. Without anthropomorphism we cannot understand what alien or animal subjectivity is. If we prohibit anthropomorphism, we block off an essential approach to our interpretation of the world.

Peter Schuster: I agree with you completely. Our everyday way of describing the world is very different from the scientific picture we make for ourselves. We pose completely different questions. If we go to a farmer and ask him what must be done to get piglets, and whether this is not an enormously difficult process, then the farmer will answer that it is not difficult at all; he just has to get a boar and bring it together with a sow, and after seven weeks he will have the piglets. He does not understand the language that the molecular biologist uses for this process. Many people believe that our everyday life can be controlled only if we use simple formulas to describe it. These descriptive formulas lead us to the goal when they are empirically well founded and phylogenetically prepared for, but often they lead us terribly astray. For example, we are very bad at estimating probabilities, whereas in other things we have developed great precision, for instance, in measuring distances and velocities. What appears simple or difficult to us in life is very much dependent on the circumstances of our evolutionary history, whereas natural science breaks out of this system.

I often discuss with a friend the notions of quantum mechanics. With respect to the problem of waves and particles, I venture to declare that we cannot imagine this. We simply have to note that our world of experience is the world that we and our ancestors have lived in and mastered. Quantum mechanics does not belong to this world of experience. Another example of this is astrophysics. Our insights into the microscopic realms of life are in a certain way a new world of this sort. And perhaps in the future we will see the question of complexity precisely as a ray of light shining into a world that was not the one from which we came phylogenetically, one in which therefore other rules applied.

Vincent Twomey: I have the impression that our discussion is being determined largely by the natural sciences. They have, so to speak, already occupied the field. We hardly spoke about theology and creation until Professor Spaemann pointed them out to us.

I was very impressed by Professor Schuster's essay, "From Belief to Facts in Evolutionary Theory", in which he discusses the clash of science and church in England when Darwin published his ideas and Bishop Wilberforce took up a position against them. The problem is, I believe, that the natural sciences from the very beginning probably had a false concept of creation, namely, that God was understood as the one who filled in the gaps. To what extent has science dealt with the idea of creation as theology actually presents it?

I have difficulties, too, with Professor Spaemann's statement that the unity of reality exists, without abandoning either side, only if we bring into play the idea of creation, according to which the process of the origin of life and of the species is founded in one and the same will of the divine wisdom. Here many questions arise: What does God's will mean? What does wisdom mean? How did the world come about? How are we to understand the relation between God and the world? The theology of Thomas Aquinas started from the contingency of the world and distinguished within the world between those things that occur by necessity and those things whose variability is built into creation.

My questions, therefore, are: First, is science interested in what theology has to say today about creation? And second, can we in fact accept this dualism about which Professor Spaemann was talking? Of course there are different kinds of knowledge, and philosophy tries to relate them, but I think we may have to go farther in this direction.

Josef Zohrer: I would like to add something here: I always have the feeling that whenever the attempt is made to bring creation theology and natural science together, people start looking for a gap in science. It has already been suggested that this cannot be the point of the matter. The question is asked how one can still accommodate belief in creation somehow, so that it can answer the question about meaning. As Siegfried Wiedenhofer has suggested in his essay "Belief in Creation and the Theory of Evolution" (see appendix, pages 177–206), in the center stands the question of a *point of intersection* between the two. Are both sides open to each other? Is there an open flank in each for the other science?

My question to Professor Schuster is whether the natural sciences take into account that there are also spiritual (immaterial) causes. Naturally the question then arises again: What is spirit? Concerning this I would like to give an example from pedagogy: I can raise children by giving them everything they need to eat and can simulate love, or I can *genuinely* love the children. Presumably they will develop very differently, although on a molecular biological level everything proceeds identically. Could such a spiritual world of a higher order, which cannot be ascertained scientifically, be a collateral cause of natural processes, or would we have to rule this out from the start?

Peter Schuster: You are asking a very difficult question for natural scientists, because the method of natural science per se is aimed at developing concepts that are verifiable by some sort of test. In this regard, Popper held the very radical view that a theory that cannot be falsified cannot be part of natural science. I do not agree with Popper's thinking in all areas, because he is drawing a picture of physics, whereas we cannot proceed in that way in other sectors of the natural sciences, in which other systems are elaborated.

I think that a distinction must be made between addressing the scientist as a man and addressing him as a scientist. If one addresses him as a scientist, then he has to hold fast to the principle that his considerations ought to be falsifiable. As far as the problem of genuine or simulated love is concerned, one must be extremely careful with the share that molecular biology contributes to it. We have just learned in recent years that many things that we imagined to have nothing to do with material processes are absolutely governed also by the chemistry of our brain. For example, scientists have discovered substances that the body releases in

certain circumstances, for instance in accidents, to anaes-
thetize pain, which is necessary to ward off dangers. Discussions about models of behavior that apply to the social
relations between parents and children are very difficult to
conduct and cannot be treated exhaustively by natural science as such. Even among animals, hormonal influences
play an important role in the behavior of mothers. Nevertheless, I would answer your question, not as a scientist,
but as a human being, with a fund of experiences drawn
from life.

I would like to address another misunderstanding here: It
is not right to say that the overwhelming majority of biologists have been or are now on the look-out for a lack of
purpose. At this juncture I would like to reply also to something that Cardinal Schönborn said. I believe that it is simply the *non-detection* of such a purpose, which has been the
case in scientific investigations, that leads us to our current
interpretation. This does not mean, however, that fifty years
from now we could not have other findings.

Naturally, the socialization and the world view of a scientist also influence the manner in which he approaches
problems. But it is a difficult enterprise to falsify the contents which happens again and again, because in science
very precise observations are made. You win a lot more
fame by disproving a theory than by corroborating it. And
so, for instance, during my student days, many scientists
were trying to disprove the theory of relativity, whereas today
there are hardly any more attempts of that sort. At the
moment we are going through a similar phase within the
natural sciences with regard to evolutionary biology. In
the last fifty years many things in biology have become much,
much clearer; even areas that we do not yet understand are
outlined with greater clarity than before. When a scientist

has a result that grossly contradicts this, it will immediately meet with approval. I do not think one can accuse scientists of being ideological or blind to certain areas. They are indeed, however, bound to their method, and, as Professor Spaemann said, this is only one part of reality.

Certainly, I was somewhat disappointed that you so strongly emphasized the impossibility of purposeful dialogue, but I can see how that follows from your point of view.

Robert Spaemann: Your distinction between "as a scientist" and "as a human being" is precisely what I meant by the two ways of seeing. Of course, I would not contrast the term "human being" with scientist, because the scientist *as* scientist is naturally a human being, too, precisely in a very particular expression of humanity. Besides this, however, there is the other, everyday approach, which scientists like to look at as something provisional, that works well enough until it has been cleared up by science. This is, so to speak, the slum neighborhood of existence that will be cleaned up someday. This view, however, in my opinion, is wrong, for the everyday approach is a *legitimate* approach that also reveals reality to us. My example for this was the fact that being as unity or subjectivity as the new unity are things to which the scientist *as* natural scientist has no access. He has access only to complexity. Since it is reality, though, that my dog is hungry, I must not wait until the scientist explains the phenomenon of hunger to me.

Another comment about the immaterial or spiritual causes: You have chosen a precarious example, because the question is to what extent one can simulate love. Let us take a much simpler example: mathematical laws. Suppose that someone has made a mathematical discovery (which cannot be traced back to natural science) and writes down the corresponding formula. Here a mathematical state of affairs, for instance, whether there can be a highest prime number (and thus a purely immaterial phenomenon that is more exact than a natural science can ever be), leads to a physical result, namely, the record of a formula.

Christoph Cardinal Schonborn: Many questions have been addressed that require further elaboration. I would like to single out two of them: On the one hand, creation theology, which we are supposed to work on further, especially in our discussion with the Holy Father. The Holy Father was and is indeed one of the few prominent theologians of the second half of the twentieth century who have warned about the deficit in creation theology, and he began very early on to counteract that trend. Many of the problems that have been brought up in today's discussion and that were already very plain to see in Darwin's writings are a result of the fact that people in those circles had a very deficient theology of creation, which was then attacked.

What challenge does that present for theology today? We need a genuine creation theology that can see eye-to-eye with the natural sciences on the intellectual level. This is the first theme on which we absolutely must focus. The second theme is the thought expressed by Professor Spaemann when he says that selfhood is emancipation from the conditions of origin. Richard Dawkins said in an interview that he would not like to live in a Darwinian world. But if everything is evolution, how can he want to live in a world that is different from the one described by those mechanisms? It is possible only because there is such a thing as emancipation from the conditions of origin. We all want this and strive for it, for example, when we distinguish between a simulated and an authentic love.

Lecture by Father Paul Erbrich, S.J.:
"The Problem of Creation and Evolution"
(see pages 70–83)

Christoph Cardinal Schonborn: Thank you, Father Erbrich, for this in-depth, intriguing lecture. I think that the first ones whom we should ask for a response are the two previous speakers.

Peter Schuster: I would like first to look at a few details more closely and then get to something more general. In talking about the concept of mechanism, you deliberately or inadvertently left out chemistry, although this term was first coined in chemistry, I think. The concept in question refers to the manner in which molecules react with one another: If I know the mechanism, I can translate the process into equations and make calculations about the chemical kinetics. From the perspective of molecular biology, the concept of mechanism must be understood in evolution as an abstract concept that describes how individuals or molecules enter into interaction with each other. A mechanism is basically an abstraction from the detailed dynamic events such as the collision of molecules, energy transfer processes, or the interaction between matter and light.

This is exactly how I understand the concept of mechanism in evolution as well, only in that context it is abstracted from the carriers, also. Whether you are dealing with molecules, organisms, or—to mention an analogy from physics—laser modes, selection always enters into the picture when there is a definite mechanism. Therefore "mechanism" is not an excuse for states of affairs that have not been understood, as I seem to have heard Mr. Erbrich imply, but rather simply a formalization of the interrelationships between units that act dynamically in a totality.

I would like to say something more about self-organization. This term is used for very different things. You can do without it, too, if you like; then you just have to classify processes in some other way. There are processes that, on the basis of their inherent dynamics, in other words, on the basis of their mechanism, lead to an equilibrium either directly or by way of intermediate steps. If you take the second law of thermodynamics seriously, this happens in all processes to which equilibrium thermodynamics applies. In contrast to this class, there is another type of processes that obey a different set of rules: As long as an energy flow continues, these processes do not go in the direction of higher entropy but rather export entropy by means of an energy flow. In the overall system—including the surroundings—the second law applies just as well, but structures emerge. The nice thing is that behind all these processes there is only one principle, namely, the principle of self-reinforcement.

One example from chemistry is the explosion. Chemical reactions go faster at a higher temperature. Therefore when the process itself produces heat, it gets even hotter even faster, and the result is self-reinforcement, even though in this case there is not much that can be called self-organization. If you heat a liquid from below, a structuring of the process develops, a convection pattern, because it has departed from the unordered state of equilibrium through the same phenomenon of self-reinforcement.

Biological systems, too, observe this fundamental principle of self-reinforcement. When organisms reproduce more quickly, there are more of them in the next generation, and the result is self-reinforcement. The big difference, in my view, is that chemical or physical processes have no memory of their past. If, for instance, a pattern develops over a certain interval, it cannot develop later once again on its own, because information about its past is lacking. In biology, in contrast, there is a recollection of the past inasmuch as information, both about the object itself and also about the machinery by which it is produced, is passed on to the next generation.

Another comment on goal-oriented activity: As an explanation for adaptation, you posit the goal-oriented action of organisms. I tried to describe an experiment in which molecules adapt to given surroundings in such an evolutionary process. I would by no means attribute goal-oriented action to these molecules; rather, they achieve the same types of adaptation that we see in nature. There is nothing mysterious about adaptations in the molecular realm, therefore; they require no additional mechanism in order to be understood.

I would like to explain something else about the leaps to which you refer. In the development of living things, especially of higher forms of life, scientists have only recently discovered the phenomenon that genetic information has been doubled. It makes sense that a marked change in the development takes place thereby. Precisely as a result of these doublings of the genome, the same molecules in higher organisms can be used for different purposes, that is, can be applied at various places in the mechanism, which finally leads, in the view of most molecular biologists, to the complexity that can be seen today. I have difficulties with any sort of goal-oriented action when I see that certain structures carry about with them a past that later proves to be to their disadvantage. I mentioned the human eye, but there are many other examples as well. If I can see as a whole the process that effects this amazing higher development, then

I do not need this goal-oriented activity of the individual organisms.

Paul Erbrich: Thank you very much, Mr. Schuster. I will begin with the doubling of the genome. Here a problem arises: Now I have the same thing twice. This occurs often among plants (polyploidy), but among (higher) animals practically never. How can the doubling of a genome produce something new (not only an improvement on what existed previously)? Apparently the one genome begins to change, while the other remains for the moment what it is, so as to be able to maintain the success that it has had thus far. Now the problem is getting a concrete idea of what such a restructuring entails. Let us take an example: over the course of their evolution, anaerobic bacteria have "learned" to absorb light and to apply the absorbed light energy in various chemical steps so as to reduce carbon dioxide and to construct their own cellular materials out of it with greater efficiency than before. How many different "unemployed" genes in the doubled genome have to be changed in order to achieve these steps? How many of them must be changed in lockstep, so as to become deployable in a helpful way (though not yet with the perfection that they have today); in lockstep because they [the improvements] are dependent on each other? It seems to me that the mechanisms that scientists have found through test-tube experiments still fall too short.

Or let us take another case: pseudo-genes. In the genomes of higher organisms there are many DNA segments that exhibit the features of genes but are never translated into what they mean, into the corresponding proteins. Therefore, they are called pseudo-genes. They are still subject to chance variation, like all genes. Therefore, they very soon lose their original information and functionality without, however, gaining a new one. For they are exempt from natural selection, since they are no longer translated. But how, then, can genes with new functions come about? Hardly through Darwin's mechanism of chance and selection alone.

I do not exactly understand why you describe mechanisms as something abstract. When I consider how chemical reactions that take place in femtoseconds are investigated today, then these mechanisms appear to me to be something very concrete. That is why I think my description is correct after all: mechanisms tell us who has an effect on what, how, and with what result. They are a form of efficient causality (*causae efficientes*). In the purely inorganic, material realm, there is no spontaneity of the sort that we quite matter-of-factly ascribe to plants and animals in the world we experience. Living things as a whole not only act in goal-oriented ways, which is obvious; they also strive for the goals. During a dry season, plants do everything possible to protect themselves from wilting. They do not do this directly and immediately, through sheer "will power", so to speak. They do it indirectly by way of efficient causes, called mechanisms. Efficient causes are the thing by which a final cause accomplishes in space and time what it is trying to achieve. That is why the body of a plant or of an animal is such an incredibly complicated piece of machinery, which we can and should investigate scientifically. Often I have the impression that natural scientists are afraid that those who speak of teleology might take their jobs away, because mechanisms then become irrelevant. Have no fear, though; there is such an incredible abundance of mechanisms that the chemists, biologists, and geologists still have enough work for decades, if not centuries! It has struck me that in articles about theoretical physics (about a field, therefore, that can be expressed thoroughly in mathematical formulas, in contrast to all the other scientific disciplines), one practically never finds the word "mechanism". Why this is so is a difficult and intriguing question.

As for self-organization: although we have a marked increase in structure and organization in organisms, the law of entropy is not violated. Here, too, entropy is generated, but it is exported, that is, the entropy in the surroundings increases. In this we agree. We also agree that structures come about through energy streams. But now if you take, for instance, the Bénard reaction or the Zhabotinsky reaction, you get very pretty things, but they have nothing to do with *purpose*fulness [*Zweckmässigkeit*], which distinguishes organic and technical structures on all levels (and which should not be confused with *goal*-oriented activity [*Zielstrebigkeit*]). If hexagonal convection cells result when a not-too-thick layer of crude oil is heated from below, no one will declare that they were produced for the purpose of dissipating the heat energy of the hotplate; that can happen by conduction, by ordered convection, or much more frequently by unordered convection. In organisms, however, there are countless purposeful, "artful" structures even in the macromolecular realm. ATP-synthetase, for example, could quite accurately be described as a machine for the production of ATP molecules. I do not see how something like that could come about through mechanisms alone.

To explain: ATP molecules are energy "packets" that the organism uses to set chemical reactions in motion. In general, a chemical synthesis requires energy, which is made available for that purpose by ATP molecules. ATP is produced in the mitochondria by the energy that the body obtains, for example, when it oxidizes sugar into carbon dioxide and water.

Peter Schuster: ATP can perhaps best be described as the energy "currency" of the body: Because it can be obtained so quickly, it can be used for a wide variety of purposes.

I think that the word "formal" that I used with reference to mechanisms was misunderstood. You were quite right in saying that I can analyze things in femtoseconds, but what I am measuring then is the kinetics. From the kinetics I must infer the mechanism, which is very simple to do in chemistry. But with the mechanism, what I am concerned about, in a merely formal way, is what molecule reacts with what, without knowing their structure. Perhaps we have misunderstood each other in this matter.

Spontaneity means that something suddenly results from something else. The Bénard phenomenon is spontaneous already in this sense, because previously I simply have heat conduction and then suddenly convection. If you point out the difference that a Zhabotinsky reaction or a Bénard phenomenon fulfills no purpose, then I would reply that in this case there is no information carrier present, either, by which it is produced and that it therefore cannot be adapted by variations but rather must develop anew each time.

Robert Spaemann: I was impressed by Father Erbrich's lecture in the way that one is impressed by things that coincide with one's own view, and I just wanted to go into one point in more detail: the problem of the beginning of teleology. Indeed, among theorists of science there is the thesis that teleology is present only where there is a consciousness and a conscious setting of a goal. Here at the beginning we are confronted with a somewhat dangerous idea, already in the writings of Thomas Aquinas, but especially *after* him. A remarkable logical conclusion is drawn here. From teleology Thomas Aquinas concludes the existence of a divine Author.

You correctly noted that one does not have to assume the existence of God in order to accept teleology, but rather vice versa: when one sees teleological phenomena, one arrives perhaps at the thought that there may have been someone who set this goal. Thomas uses the image of the arrow and the marksman. In his opinion, teleology is not in the arrow, but in the marksman, and from this he makes a proof for the existence of God. This is not quite in keeping with Aristotle, who says that teleology is most obvious or most tangible where it is without consciousness. The flute player who no longer has to reflect is the better flute player. This leads, then, in the writings of Jean Buridan, to the opinion that one must understand the world in a purely causal and mechanical way; that there is a divine architect who has introduced a goal that is nonetheless not immanent in things.

I wanted to ask the question: Where does teleology begin? In my opinion, one cannot begin with man. After all, we discover our own needs even before we set goals. We allow our needs to specify the goals for us, for instance, when we are hungry. What reason should we have for not assuming the existence of teleology in earlier, less complex organisms? Where does real goal-oriented activity begin? Does it suddenly fall from the sky? Ultimately it cannot have developed out of non-teleological structures.

Paul Erbrich: I would like to hear how you, Mr. Spaemann, show that teleological behavior cannot arise from a-teleological behavior. To me, it stands to reason, and I think that this can be demonstrated plausibly in several ways. One problem perhaps lies in the fact that we still have to say that fundamentally every reality is striving for something: Omne agens agit propter finem (Everything that acts, acts for the sake of an end). If that is true, one must assume that there is a striving toward goals in inanimate matter, too, for example, toward an equilibrium.

Peter Schuster: If we furnish all processes with goals, then the goal is ultimately reduced to the result of change. Then the concept dissolves and must be specified anew, which in this context has already happened to some extent with the distinction between goals of lower and higher valence.

*Paul Erbrich:** Natural scientists often and without hesitation talk about the *tendency* of material systems toward states of decreased internal energy and greater entropy, that is, to states of greater probability. It is striving toward the Dead Point, at which nothing new happens any more. Unlike what you find in the realm of living things, a wide variety of material systems all have the same goal, the Dead Point; this is in contrast to the organic realm, where there are as many specifically different goals as there are different species (sparrows pursue other goals than intestinal bacteria). Concretely, of course, the Dead Point may look quite different in certain cases for various systems (one way for the Matterhorn and another way for Sirius). But what is different is not striven for as something different, but only because it is the Dead Point that is attainable here and now. Furthermore it is reached directly, without assistance. Purely material systems require no "artful", purposeful structures (for example, enzymes or apparatus for movement) in order to reach the goal of the Dead Point.

---

* The next three speeches were reconstructed by Father Erbrich from memory. The summary of the remarks by Robert Spaemann was approved by the latter.

Robert Spaemann: There can be a real striving, a genuine "being out for something", only toward something that is itself also real (or at least really possible). A Dead Point (actually a Nothing) is not worth being striven for and is not capable of it, either.

Paul Erbrich: "Dead Point" is actually too dramatic an expression and therefore misleading. More objectively I should say: stable equilibrium. In a system that is in equilibrium, many and varied things can happen, but always the same things, no longer anything new. It is stable when it has reached a state where it can be changed only from outside. Above all, it is an endpoint rather than a goal (as death is for all living things). The headlong rush of inanimate systems toward this endpoint, however, has a meaning (and therefore can be a goal): Like the rush of water from a reservoir into the valley, it provides the energy that helps living things to resist the "pounding surf of entropy", to multiply and to climb ever higher on the evolutionary ladder up to the (provisional?) endpoint "man", an enfleshed spirit living in the world.

Robert Spaemann: One could call technomorphic findings "anthropocentric" as well. We face the alternative of thinking either anthropocentrically or anthropomorphically. The former would mean relating everything to us and to our purposes, whereby it is important to leave aside proper purposes in nature. Francis Bacon once said that the observation of things under the aspect of their orientation toward a goal is like a consecrated virgin who gives birth to nothing. The anthropomorphic way of thinking, in contrast, observes everything outside ourselves under the aspect that it is somehow similar to us. The *res cogitans* [thing that thinks] and the *res extensa* [thing having extension] are, indeed, separated by a chasm, but it is interesting that Descartes eliminates "life" from the classical triad: being—life—consciousness. Life, he maintains, is an unclear idea. In order to have clear ideas, one must restrict oneself to consciousness and objective being. The reason why the concept of life is bothersome here is because it brings us into an association with everything living. And this way of thinking can be called anthropomorphic. I would not regard anthropomorphism as a reproach. Nietzsche quite correctly recognizes that even our concept of a thing as a unity is anthropomorphic. He says that we must give up the idea of "the thing as a unity" as a final anthropomorphism, for the fact that we understand ourselves as a unity is an illusion. In reality, there are no unities at all, but only a Heraclitean stream in which one can no longer identify anything.

Christoph Cardinal Schonborn: We conclude our discussion today with many thanks to our three speakers for their impressive presentations.

September 2, Morning

Repetition of the lecture by Peter Schuster:
"Evolution and Design" (see pages 27–60)

Pope Benedict XVI: Many thanks, Professor Schuster. With your "song" you have managed to give, even to people who are rather unmusical in this field, some notion of the great and complex mystery of nature. We are very grateful to you that we have had at least this glimpse "from afar", which makes clear to us the limit of our knowledge, yet also shows—as you suggested at the conclusion—that one can discern even greater things behind it.

Repetition of the lecture by Robert Spaemann: "Common Descent and Intelligent Design" (see pages 61–69)

Pope Benedict XVI: Professor Spaemann, you have told us things that are profound and at the same time things that are amusing and concrete as well. You have defused our potential quarrel by warning us against premature alliances and tell us: It is not yet time to reconcile the two realms. We are glad to hear this message. I have always been of the opinion that overhasty attempts at harmonization are usually not very durable. At the conclusion, however, you also pointed out to us that we must not stop making the attempt to unite the two worlds and to see behind them which code supports the whole, even though we could not arrive at a harmonization.

Christoph Cardinal Schonborn: I have a critical question for Professor Schuster. I am very glad that scientists today consider Darwin's theory of the small steps to be an error, that they can toss it, so to speak, onto the dust heap of the history of theories. Now, however, it only matters as a typical example of something that I have noted and criticized again and again: for decades anyone who called into question the theory of the small steps was very severely punished. Father Erbrich has researched this and has published a study on how this theory, *lege artis* [by the rules of the discipline], leads one to a dead end. I am one of those people who regard it as impossible based on philosophical considerations. I cannot judge it from a scientific perspective, but in light of natural philosophy one must say: It cannot be that development took place through small steps. Now we are confronted with the fact that the natural scientists have shelved this theory. But there is no *poenitentia* [repentance], so to speak, for having scolded those who had their doubts about it even earlier. Excuse me, if I have expressed myself somewhat polemically, but I think that this situation shows how difficult it is, now as before, to raise objections against the prevailing theory, especially in the study of the origin of life. It is all the more encouraging to note that today these objections are seen as justified within science itself.

Vincent Twomey: At the end of your lecture, Professor Schuster, it became clear to me that there is perhaps after all a glimmer of hope for a union between natural science and philosophy, or else theology. You said that in their observations of the entire universe, from the Big Bang down to the present time, scientists have found a line between chaos and order that could be a sign of the Creator. Could you tell me something more precise about this? It struck me that, despite the multiplicity of sciences, we basically know very little, and, secondly, that where living things are concerned, you have excluded teleology and admitted teleonomy. But in the final analysis are these two concepts not the same? For example, if you have a zygote made up of semen and egg, a process begins that is much greater than what is present in the genes themselves. And so something else must be there in addition. Could this reflection not be extrapolated to the cosmos as well?

Peter Schuster: I will begin with an answer to Cardinal Schönborn. The reason why Darwin assumed the notion of small steps was because he wanted to oppose very deliberately the catastrophe theorists of the early nineteenth century. The combination of the Darwinian principle of natural selection with Mendelian heredity already determined that the steps cannot become infinitely small. For if such elements of heredity exist, then a change in these elements will effect some difference or other. By its very nature, the difference will always be discrete; only its consequence for the selection process can become infinitesimal. The discrete character of hereditary genetics is probably one of many reasons why the Mendelian concepts were at first not accepted at all in the world of biologists. We must not forget that in the late nineteenth and early twentieth century, Boltzmann had tremendous difficulties gaining acceptance for the concept of the atom in physics. The small steps were quantized, so to speak, by the Mendelian concepts. For a long time there was the idea that, when we go from the genes to the phenotypes, we can have arbitrarily small gradations. But that was given up, too. Phenotypes exist in the world that are practically continuous, for example body size, but with many other qualities this is not the case. It is an instance of progress in science that today we no longer feel that these small steps are a must. They can occur now and then, but in principle there is a quantization of the characteristics.

Probably in the very near future it will also happen that scientists manage to understand better the development of the organism from the fertilized egg cell—and with that, I would like to address the second question. Then we will find there further steps that are necessarily discrete.

The "punishment" of scientists who have put up resistance to the accepted views is found all through science, and it is no less common in the dispute between natural science and theology or between science and philosophy. There are quotations that show how Mendel's followers insulted the natural selectionists, and vice versa. Shortly before the development of the synthetic theory, when the population geneticists were already able to unify their theory on the mathematical level, one biologist asked, "Where have we arrived in biology? We have two methodologies that for twenty-five years have been arguing intransigently with each other." But then there was a solution *within* natural science.

In relation to the question of what is already present in the genes for the coming development, I made a remark that is very important in this connection: If I take the genetic information only as a nucleic acid molecule, then there is nothing at all present in it, because with all the possibilities that are available to me, I can only read off a very limited section of its agenda and timetable. Whereas I can transform individual segments into proteins with techniques that we still did not have twenty or thirty years ago, even with all our knowledge today I cannot produce a cell in this manner, nor can I trace the developmental biology.

You may ask how everything can be contained in this little piece of information. Here it is significant that the ovum, too, brings along an essential part of the information that is necessary for the development. This was always termed "epigenesis", that is, what "stands behind" or supports genetics. Of course, scientists knew that not everything can be determined by the genes. But the really new thing is that we know the manner in which this other determination takes place.

The question, though, I think, was more about how the entire development can be encoded in such a gene. Here the metaphor of a computer program is helpful, although naturally it, too, limps. What is encoded in the gene are the individual commands of a program that is started in the interaction between the ovum and the genetic information. The ovum is, so to speak, the necessary hardware. Even with the computer, after all, the program is extremely small in relation to the operations that it carries out. One can imagine the development of an organism in a similar way: Certain genetically encoded signals are given, whereupon development processes take place that can be understood in terms of the cell's overall metabolism.

September 2, Afternoon

Repetition of the lecture by Father Paul Erbrich, S.J.:
"The Problem of Creation and Evolution"
(see pages 70–83)

Pope Benedict XVI: Father Erbrich, you have informed
us about a lot of things and given us much to think about.
And now comes the lecture by Cardinal Schönborn as the
grand finale. We are looking forward to it.

Repetition of the lecture by Christoph Cardinal
Schönborn: *Fides, Ratio, Scientia* (see pages 84–106)

Pope Benedict XVI: Our sincere thanks, Your Eminence;
you have not only enlightened our understanding but also
touched our hearts.

With the four lectures that we have heard, we are faced
now with a very broad spectrum that we could discuss for
a very long time; unfortunately, though, we have only a
little time available to do so. After the break we can consider a few more questions. I think that above all the speakers themselves want to say something to each other, for
each other, but also against each other, but always in the

productive adversarial relationship that aims at recognizing the truth and assuming responsibility for it.

We must consider what we want to do with the treasure of these four lectures. Perhaps they, too, have a *telos*. It seems to me that it was providence that led you, Your Eminence, to write an opinion piece for *The New York Times*, to make this topic current again and to show what the real issues are: that it is not a question of deciding either for a creationism that is closed off from science as a matter of principle, or else for a theory of evolution that has its own gaps and yet overplays its hand and is unwilling to look at the questions that go beyond the methodological possibilities of the natural sciences. Rather, it is a question precisely of this *interplay* of the various dimensions of reason, in which the path to faith opens up as well. If between *ratio* and *fides* you emphasize *scientia* or *philosophia*, then what is fundamentally at stake is regaining a dimension of reason that we have lost. Without that dimension, faith would be confined to a ghetto and thus lose its significance for the whole of reality and of human existence.

The lectures we have heard today have to some extent gone beyond what I am saying now, because it developed directly from listening to the lecture by Professor Schuster, but I would like to say it anyway. You, dear Sir, Professor Schuster, have in the first place impressively shown the logic of the developing theory of evolution, which gradually leads to a large conceptual context, and have pointed out also the internal corrections (especially to Darwin's ideas) that were discovered along the way. In the second place, you have very clearly set forth the questions that remain open. Not as if I wanted now to cram the dear Lord into these gaps: He is too great to be able to find lodgings in such gaps. But it seems to me important to underscore that the theory of evolution implies questions that must be assigned to philosophy and that in and of themselves lead beyond the internal scope of the natural sciences.

In particular, to me it is important, first of all, that to a great extent the theory of evolution cannot be proved experimentally, quite simply because we cannot bring 10,000 generations into the laboratory. That means that there are considerable gaps in its experimental verifiability and falsifiability due to the enormous span of time to which the theory has reference.

A second thing that was important to me was your statement that the probability is not zero, but not one, either. And so the question arises: How high *is* the probability now? This is important especially if we want to interpret correctly the remark by Pope John Paul II: "The theory of evolution is more than a hypothesis." When the Pope said that, he had his reasons. But at the same time it is true that the theory of evolution is still not a complete, scientifically verified theory.

Third, I would like to address the leaps, which Cardinal Schönborn also spoke about. The summing up of minute steps does not suffice. There are "leaps". The question of what this involves has to be examined in greater detail.

The fourth interesting thing is that the positive mutations are few and the corridor in which the development was able to play itself out is narrow. This corridor was actually opened up and walked through. Science itself and the theory of evolution can explain many things impressively, but the four points just mentioned show that there are also major unanswered questions.

Before I come to the logical conclusion that I draw from this, I would like to say something that Cardinal Schönborn, too, has already addressed: Not only popular writing about science, but also scholarly scientific texts about evolution often say that "nature" or "evolution" did this or that. Here the question arises: Who in fact is "Nature" or "Evolution" as an acting subject? There is no such person! If someone says that Nature does this or that, this can only be an attempt to summarize a series of processes in a subject that, however, does not exist as such. It seems obvious to me that this (perhaps indispensable) linguistic expedient contains within it momentous questions.

In summary, I would like to say that science has opened up major dimensions of reason that previously had not been accessible and have thereby provided us with new knowledge. But in its joy over the greatness of its discoveries, it tends to confiscate dimensions of our reason that we still need. Its findings lead to questions that reach beyond its methodological principles and cannot be answered within science itself. Nevertheless these are questions that reason must ask itself and that must not simply be left to religious feeling. We must look at them as reasonable questions and also find reasonable ways of dealing with them.

These are the great perennial questions of philosophy, which confront us in a new way: the question of where man and the world come from and where they are going. Apropos of this, I recently became aware of two things that the three following lectures also made clear: There is, in the first place, a rationality of matter itself. One can read it. It has mathematical properties; matter itself is rational, even though there is much that is irrational, chaotic, and destructive on the long path of evolution. But matter per se is legible. Secondly, it seems to me that the process, too, as a whole, has a rationality about it. Despite its false starts and meanderings through the narrow corridor, the process as such is something rational in its selection of the few positive mutations and in its exploitation of the minute probabilities. This twofold rationality, which in turn proves to correspond to our human reason, unavoidably leads to a question that goes beyond science yet is a reasonable question: Where does this rationality originate? Is there an originating rationality that is reflected in these two zones and dimensions of rationality? Science cannot and must not answer this question directly, but we should acknowledge that the question is a reasonable one and dare to believe in the creative Reason and to entrust ourselves to It. This, if you do not mind, is the little bundle of questions that I wanted to pose to you.

Peter Schuster: Thank you very much, Holy Father. I would like to reply to a few things that you have very precisely noted. The theory of evolution is a science in progress, and it can only be in progress if there are still unanswered questions. If all the questions are answered, then a science lies there dead, so to speak, and cannot develop further.

I think that people require more from the theory of evolution in this respect than they do from other theories. I take as an example quantum physics, which contains some phenomena that are difficult to imagine, such as the Einstein-Podolsky-Rosen phenomenon, which states that elementary particles having a common origin always know about each other, even if they are far removed. Einstein posited this as a paradox, and nevertheless quantum physics was accepted as a theory. It was not until seventy years later, in the 1990s, that someone was able to demonstrate through an experiment that this in fact happens, even though to us it seems counterintuitive.

We cannot perform experiments that take eons, as you correctly noted, nor will we able to do so in the future. I have tried to show that we can still use another dimension, too, which consists of the fact that we carry in our genetic material a memory of our past. The interpretation of this material makes this second approach possible for us.

Gaps there are, and you have rightly asked about the big steps in evolution. The last of these big steps is the transition from animal societies to human societies. The others concern biological details, for instance, the transition from one-celled to multi-celled organisms or from individual animals to animal colonies with complex caste structures such as we find among ants and bees. Then there is also, for example, the transition from a world in which the genetic material was concentrated only in the nucleic acids, that is, in RNA molecules, to our present world with DNA and protein. In all, eight such stages can be distinguished.

With reference to probability, I wanted to make another short remark: We know nothing about these probabilities. The statement that it is between zero and one is of course trivial. We can begin, however, by investigating mutations at least locally, as is possible for simple organisms. I am very glad, Holy Father, that you have taken up the point at which I stepped out of the scientific field: the narrow corridor. The laws of nature studied by physicists contain certain constants of nature. If these laws of nature were to be there in an only slightly modified form, the world would have developed in a completely different manner. Even at the planetary stage, very special conditions are required, for example, if water is to be a liquid, in order to make possible life as we know it. With respect to life as well, the area between order and chaos is such a narrow corridor. If we look now at the process as a whole, this long corridor from the Big Bang through the origin of life down to the origin of man, then this testifies, I think, to a plan that I do not find in science, which of course observes the individual processes. This corridor can be the work of a Creator.

Johannes Lehmann-Dronke: I would like to add a few reflections to the remarks thus far in the lectures and in the contributions to the discussions.* It is striking that all theories of evolution start from the assumption, which is regarded as self-evident, that all material things, since they consist of certain "fundamental building blocks" (energy quanta, elementary particles, atoms, molecules), are constructed according to a sort of "modular construction principle" and should be understood accordingly. On the basis of the laws proper to these "building blocks", it is supposed, the variety of the whole material world develops through their self-organization under conditions suitable for the required reactions. According to this view, no really new thing can exist, only an increasing complexity in the mutual association of the "building blocks". What always manifests itself in such a so-called "higher development" of the given material realities is only something that is already present, in changing phenomenal forms.

On the contrary, in today's scientific view, the material world cannot be described according to a "modular construction principle". Rather, all material compounds are totalities that cannot be explained solely from the peculiar structure of their "building blocks". Even though their "building blocks" are disposed to entering into particular complex compounds, the peculiar structure of those components does not contain the program for what has thereby come to be, in its totality and unity. This finding impinges

---

* What follows is a subsequent expansion of the original contribution to the discussion.

less on the awareness of the natural scientist, because he is accustomed to understanding and describing the elemental "building blocks" of matter quantitatively, in a functional concurrence or collaboration, that is, starting from wholes and then proceeding to the discovery of their peculiar structures.

The epistemological path, therefore, goes from the functional connections in the systems at hand to the discovery of the peculiar structure of the "building blocks", which scientists can then make use of in reverse for chemical synthesis procedures. An understanding, obtained in this way, of the emergence of other systems should not, however, blind us to the fact that this still does not amount to a reasoned explanation for their peculiar character as wholes. Granted, the scientist is not accustomed to asking about what is; instead, he asks about what happens. Nevertheless, if we are concerned about understanding the material world in a discerning way, can the matter simply rest there?

Every molecule turns out, in the current view, to be an overall energy state in which each of the atoms is a carrier of the whole molecule in its entirety and unity, and not just a part thereof. Molecules are not strings of atoms, but rather interactions among them, in which each atom contributes to the formation of the overall energy state—that is, the molecule as a genuine whole.

Let us illustrate this with an example: Even the very simply structured benzene molecule is more than an array or assembly of six carbon and six hydrogen atoms. Granted, the latter by their peculiar structure (nuclear composition and electron configuration) are disposed to enter into the compound "benzene molecule" and thereby to arrive at a special, low-energy state. Nevertheless, the peculiar structure of these atoms, in their nuclear composition and electron configuration, contains within it no programming at all for the peculiar structure of the benzene molecule as a whole. With reference still to the example of the benzene molecule, an objection could be made as follows: Since hydrogen and carbon atoms, due to their peculiar structure, are disposed to form benzene molecules, the origin of the latter has been sufficiently explained after all. In certain reactive or environmental conditions, therefore, the formation of benzene will occur sometime and somewhere in the statistical play of matter. As dubious as this thesis would be in the first place, it nevertheless contributes nothing to a solution of the problem as stated here. For thereby we would be addressing only the actual occurrence and formation of benzene, but not its structure as a unity and a whole, which was at issue here. The remark that molecules, as overall energy states, can be adequately described and thus explained by the quantum field theory is no objection either. For if molecules can be described by means of quantum field theory or a multiple-particle quantum mechanics as overall energy states in which each atom is a carrier of the whole molecule and not just a part thereof, then that substantiates the above-mentioned theory about molecules as wholes that are more than the sum of their component parts.

To summarize: The entire material world is not built up according to a "modular construction principle". Every complex material compound proves to be a whole that cannot be derived from the peculiar structure of the component parts of which it is built. Some new autonomous thing comes about when autonomous "building blocks", reacting according to their own laws, are joined together to make a new chemical compound.

This holistic structure of all material things must, in my opinion, be discussed in connection with our inquiry into creation and evolution, since it calls the fundamental assumption of evolutionary theories into question. A few reflections on this, which of course in the interests of brevity can only be formulated as theses: The determination of the material world by its own inner laws is by no means in opposition to the Christian belief in creation. This determination, rather, is to be interpreted as the hallmark and demonstration of its divine origin. Our continual experience in technology and art shows that man, by personal causality (that is, human decision and intellectual effort) methodically avails himself of the interplay of the laws of nature that he has discovered. This availability of material conditions, as they are determined by their inner laws, for personal, creative causation is one of the foundations of our entire civilization. Since the determination of matter by its own inner laws is patently disposed to be availed of in rational, creative ways, the idea suggests itself that it has its origin in a creative, rational arrangement or order and furthermore manifests the continual influence of that order which keeps it in existence. It is evident that such a "creative, reasonable order" would produce no chaos; instead, it would cause selfhood, individual life, individual being to come about—down to the determination of all material things by their own inner laws. Otherwise, the availability of the material world for free, intellectual, creative working would not be possible. With sheer chance nothing can be built up and ordered.

One interpretation views the determination of matter by its own inner laws as matter's process of self-composition—the logically resulting consequence being that one has to define its empirically observable availability for reason-driven, that is, intellectual working as a small, hidden stream that forms part of that self-composition process; in my opinion, this interpretation would be a hypothesis that is hardly demonstrable using the scientific method. If, on the other hand, in the material goings-on of our world, new autonomous material realities, which react with one another according to their own laws, always come to light by being constructed out of previously existing "building blocks" (reacting with one another according to their own laws), in such a fashion that the new thing as a phenomenal whole cannot be derived from the inner laws determining what existed earlier, then in my opinion a creative, reasonable influence is to be discerned therein. Then what happens is not an automatic building up of the material structure like a jigsaw puzzle out of parts ready-made for assembly, not a self-organization of matter out of elementary particles or energy quanta; rather, something non-derivably new is built up out of what previously existed and joins into a meaningful overall context with the rest.

Because of their self-restriction to what is in fact present and accessible to quantitative measurement, the natural sciences can, using their methodological approach, neither ask about a personal cause for our material world nor verify or falsify statements on this subject. Nor are they in a position to give an interpretation for the empirically observable fact of the peculiar being and lawfulness of matter. They can merely make use of it. Demonstrated scientific findings, however, in my opinion, compellingly lead to the question for the entire material world—and not just with regard to the animated world and man—as to the traces of divine working, or, in other words, the question about its reality as creation.

Siegfried Wiedenhofer: I have a follow-up question on the lecture by Cardinal Schönborn. I must mention beforehand that I am in complete agreement with the overall purpose of it: with the critique of ideological forms of science, with the need to bring the reasonableness of the faith into play and with the mediating function of philosophy. But still I would like to put a different emphasis on one point: If I have understood correctly the main argument, it aims to show that the reasonableness of faith is proved by its success in making evident the reality of the world in its ordered structure, which cannot be explained exclusively by reasons from evolutionary theory. At the conclusion, then, the problem of theodicy is mentioned, which automatically limits this strategy again and which ultimately can be resolved only in a theological manner. I think, however, that one should not seek the reasonableness of faith in a possibly intensive or extensive ordered structure of the world—in the fact that everything runs well, so to speak. Precisely because that is in fact not the case, one should not overstrain the argument from the order of creation. It is no doubt a part of the Christian tradition; it must not be isolated, however, from the other parts and therefore must not be completely set free from the place in which it is embedded within soteriology, which views creation as being in the power of the Evil One.

For this reason I think that one should see the reasonableness of faith, not in an orderly arrangement that is as optimal as possible, but rather in the fact that faith succeeds in comprehending the world, with all its contradictions, in terms of the conditions for its potential. In this way, soteriology and the problem of theodicy are included from the start in the belief in creation.

Theo Schafer: I liked very much the way that Professor Schuster emphasized the corridor. This made clear to me the modesty of natural science, and I conclude from it also that man cannot discern the overall plan because he is an integral component of the whole. Man seems to me to be like an aphid that cannot survey the whole at all.

Christoph Cardinal Schonborn: Part of the answer to Siegfried Wiedenhofer surely lies in the reference to contingency, which perhaps received inadequate treatment in our reflections and certainly represents a theme for discussion within the theory of evolution: To what extent, if at all, is contingency taken into account in the question of "survival"? The catastrophe with the dinosaurs is definitely not part of a plan. The fact that an asteroid hit the earth and therefore 90 percent of the species are thought to have gone extinct is not part of the plan of evolution. Many, many elements in this process are contingent, and it needs to be evaluated whether it was really always a "survival of the fittest", or whether a particular living thing simply happened to be in exactly the right niche and therefore survived. Why did I survive, while my companion died? Contingency! And so we cannot relate the history of evolution, as reported in the "Darwinian story", as if it were a coherent account and impose it on all schoolchildren as the alternative to the biblical account, for the development from the worm to *homo sapiens* did not run so smoothly but rather is bound up with a great deal that is contingent.

We do not know the overall plan, yet (and this is a very sensible way of looking at it) faith—especially in the Resurrection—reveals to us a horizon of meaning that naturally presupposes belief in a Creator, whose plans are not our plans and whose thoughts are not our thoughts. But we can discern bits of his thoughts, and we can rely on his overall design: "questo progetto intelligente che è il cosmo" (this intelligent design which is the cosmos), about which the Holy Father spoke. More we cannot do, but we do not have to, either.

This critique applies not only to theology but is also addressed to the history of evolution. For if someone tries too hard to view that history as coherent, he runs the same risk as someone who thinks he knows the secret behind God's plan.

Pope Benedict XVI: The asteroid that killed so many species, then, would correspond more or less to Dr. Dupont's hammer, which just happened to fall down and smashed his head!

I would like to comment briefly on your argument, Mr. Wiedenhofer. I would not bet on the ability of faith alone to explain the whole. I believe that the two things belong together: on the one hand, there is the rationality of matter, which opens a window onto the *Creator Spiritus*. We should not let this fall by the wayside. It is the biblical belief in creation that showed us the way to a civilization of reason, which of course also has the potential to destroy itself again. That is the one dimension that has to remain, which I also call a tangential area between the Greek and the biblical world views that had to fuse the two with an inner law and an inner necessity.

Yet, on the other hand, we must also see the limits. Of course there is rationality in nature, but it does not allow us to gain a comprehensive insight into God's plan. What remain, then, are contingency and the riddle of the terrible element in nature, as Reinhold Schneider, for instance, described it after a visit to the Museum of Natural Science in Vienna. (I, too, once visited that museum with my brother, and we were aghast at so many terrible things in nature.) Despite the rationality that exists, we can observe a component of terror, which cannot be further analyzed philosophically. Here philosophy calls for something more, and faith shows us the *Logos*, who is creative reason and who incredibly at the same time was able to become flesh, to die and to rise again. With that, a completely different face of the *Logos* is manifested from what we can manage to glimpse on the basis of a groping reconstruction of the fundamental reasons for nature. The two sides of the Greek soul, too, point to this: on the one hand—great philosophy; on the other hand—tragedy, which ultimately remains unanswered. Cardinal Schönborn and Mr. Wiedenhofer should therefore join forces in order to find a common perspective.

APPENDIX

This essay by Siegfried Wiedenhofer, which was given as a lecture on October 12, 2005, as part of the philosophical congress [Philosophische Woche] sponsored by the Catholic Academy in Bavaria on the theme of "The New Debate about Evolution", was available in Castel Gandolfo in manuscript form.

Siegfried Wiedenhofer

Belief in Creation and the Theory of Evolution: Distinction and Point of Intersection

I

Preliminary Remarks

The theological definition of the relation between belief in creation and the theory of evolution faces a twofold problem today. On the one hand, creation theology—despite an abundance of essays and a whole series of summaries in handbook style—is in a state of upheaval. This upheaval also has to do with the fact that the dogmatic exposition of the Christian belief in creation takes place now ever more decisively and directly in the context of the scientific understanding of the world. On the other hand, we find not simply the unity of the scientific understanding of the world, but a multiplicity of divergent disciplines, approaches, theories, and hypotheses. Finally, even the philosophical concepts and ideas that are used as a mediating authority can be of very heterogeneous provenance. Hence every definition of this relation must place its methodological assumptions on the table beforehand.

As far as my guiding dogmatic methodology is concerned, I follow here in principle the classic Catholic dogmatic methodology,[1] which is ultimately derived from the structure of the Christian creed. According to this methodology, an article or a testimony of the Christian faith, for instance the belief in creation, is understood correctly when it is understood (1) in keeping with the "system" of the Christian faith, (2) in keeping with the "way" of the faith, and (3) in keeping with reason. Because of time limitations I must be very selective, and so I will suggest rather than enlarge upon the first two steps and then concentrate on the third step.

As for the philosophical or theoretical side of my dogmatic reflection, my presentation of creation theology will make use mainly of reflections from transcendental philosophy, in the form that Richard Schaeffler has given them in his transcendental theory of experience.[2]

2

Belief in Creation Is in Keeping with the Fundamental Structure of the Christian Faith

The Christian creed, as a rule of faith, is an affirmation of the triune God. Christians experience the one God in such diversity that the profession has to start three times, as an affirmation of God the Father, the Son, and the Holy Spirit,

[1] On this subject, see the summary by Siegfried Wiedenhofer, "Hermeneutik III. Systematisch-theologisch", in *Lexikon für Theologie und Kirche*, 3rd ed. (1996), 5:6–7. Also Walter Kasper, "Dogmatik als Wissenschaft: Versuch einer Neubegründung", *Theologische Quartalschrift* 157 (1977): 189–203.

[2] Richard Schaeffler, *Erfahrung als Dialog mit der Wirklichkeit: Eine Untersuchung zur Logik der Erfahrung* (Freiburg and Munich, 1995); Richard Schaeffler, *Philosophische Einübung in die Theologie*, vols. 1–3 (Freiburg and Munich, 2004).

or, as one might say, of "God over us", of "God with us", and of "God in us".

Behind this fundamental logic of the Christian faith stands not only the three-dimensional structure of man (natural being, historical being, spiritual being), but also—connected with this—the triad of the foundational media and loci of religious experience (cosmos, history, psyche). Secondly, Christians experience and acknowledge God as the Creator, Redeemer, and Perfecter of the world and of history. In this context, faith appears as the way between God and man, as the way from creation to perfection, at the midpoint of which stands the affirmation of Christ, because in Jesus Christ the eschatological and hence definitive sign of revelation and salvation is experienced and acknowledged. Finally, in the unity of God as well as in the difference-unity of creation, redemption, and perfection, we find, thirdly, the reason for the unity of truth and also for a final unity of faith and reason, which is why the exposition of the faith with a view to its rationality and comprehensibility constitutes a further step of the dogmatic method.

2.1 Belief in Creation in Keeping with the "System" of the Christian Faith

Actually, in Christian dogmatic theology today, there is still a far-reaching consensus[3] that belief in creation should be

[3] See Jürgen Moltmann, *The Trinity and the Kingdom: The Doctrine of God*, trans. Margaret Kohl (New York: Harper and Row, 1981); Wolfhart Pannenberg, *Systematic Theology*, trans. Geoffrey W. Bromiley (Grand Rapids, Mich.: Eerdmans, 1991), 2:1–174; Jürgen Moltmann, *God in Creation: A New Theology and the Spirit of God* (San Francisco: Harper and Row, 1985), 72–104; Hans Kessler, "Gott, der kosmische Prozess und die Freiheit: Vorentwurf einer transzendentaldialogischen Schöpfungstheologie", in *Gott, der Kosmos und die*

expounded in the first place in terms of trinitarian theology, that is, within the framework of the profession of faith in the triune God.

Reduced to its essentials, it is evident that: Belief in creation is a central experiential dimension of the Christian faith, which in one respect (difference of fundamental religious experiences) is to be distinguished from the two other dimensions (redemption and perfection), yet in another respect (the unity of God) interferes with them, inasmuch as it explains them and is explained by them. Seen from the perspective of the christological center of the experience of God, this results in the further personalization, in a more soteriological form, of the Creator God (the Father of Jesus Christ) and also of the divine power that fills us interiorly (the Holy Spirit as Person and Creator of the new creation). On the other hand, the experience of Christ and the profession of faith in Christ are explained in terms of the other two articles: Jesus Christ appears as the mediator of creation and as Jesus Christ in us (or as the spirit of Jesus Christ) and before us (his Second Coming and perfection). Analogous things are true of our experience of the Holy Spirit: The Holy Spirit appears as the Creator Spirit and the Redeemer Spirit. Seen in turn from the perspective of the affirmation of God the Father, Jesus Christ becomes

Freiheit: Biologie, Philosophie und Theologie in Gespräch, ed. Gotthard Fuchs and Hans Kessler, 200–211 (Würzburg, 1996); Gisbert Greshake, *Der dreieine Gott: Eine trinitarische Theologie*, 2nd ed. (Freiburg, 1997), 219–325; Georg Kraus, *Welt und Mensch: Lehrbuch zur Schöpfungslehre* (Frankfurt am Main, 1997), 181–216; Colin E. Gunton, *The Triune Creator: A Historical and Systematic Study* (Grand Rapids, Mich.: Eerdmans, 1998); Hans Kessler, "Schöpfung V. Systematisch-theologisch", in *Lexikon für Theologie und Kirche*, 3rd ed. (Freiburg, 2000), 9:232–33; Franz Gruber, *Im Haus des Lebens: Eine Theologie der Schöpfung* (Regensburg, 2001), 175–233.

the Son of God and the Holy Spirit becomes the Spirit of God. Not only the historical belief in redemption but also the hope of perfection can be explained and grounded in terms of the belief in creation: The hope of redemption and the hope of perfection can draw their assurance from the omnipotence of the Creator God. On the other hand, the hope of perfection is already present in creation (paradise) and in salvation history (beginning of the end times). Finally, creation appears not only "in the beginning", but also as a new creation in the history of redemption (Christians as a "new creation" in Jesus Christ and in the Holy Spirit) and in perfection (the creation of a new heavens and a new earth).

In this respect, even the first creation (as, for instance, in the apocalyptic interpretation) can be understood as a complete wreck and the passage to the new creation can be seen as the death of the old one. In this way, the belief in creation is a central part of the basic Christian experience. Like the latter, it is complex in form and very closely connected with the other dimensions of the faith. By no means is it concerned only with a beginning of the world.

Within the framework of this trinitarian exposition of the belief in creation, the question of the motive or reason for creation (why God created the world) is answered today in a fairly uniform way: freely, out of love and goodness. If the trinitarian profession of faith in God is ultimately only the expression of the basic Christian experience that God is, in himself, life, love, communion, communication, dialogue, exchange, fellowship, solidarity, then creation is a work of this love *ad extra* [outside the Trinity], free self-communication, self-giving, and gift, free expression and self-emptying of the overflowing, infinite love and goodness that make up

God's essence. Thus creation is fundamentally defined by goodness, wholeness, and freedom. It is a free share and participation in God's love, goodness, and glory and in the fullness of his life and being.

2.2 Belief in Creation in Keeping with the Way of the Christian Faith

Every faith testimony is a sign of God's revelation only insofar as it is part of the christologically and temporally structured overall way of the faith. If this is true, then the ability of the Church's faith to be explained and to bear witness is proved chiefly by the fact that the witness to the origin (and, derivatively, the tradition thus far as well) and the present situation (and indirectly future expectations also) can effectively be interpreted by each other, that is, the creative, redemptive, and perfecting presence of God within today's world is discovered and identified inasmuch as this presence is interpreted in the light of the normative faith experiences of the faith community (above all in light of the gospel of Jesus Christ), and the universal meaning of the historical promises and testimonies is discovered inasmuch as they are interpreted anew in the light of present secular and spiritual experiences. Of course this way cannot be traced step by step here. A few exemplary remarks must suffice.

With regard to the history of its structure, the way of the faith manifests a process of repeated differentiation. That is why the special character of the Christian idea of creation can really be brought out only through a contrast with the alternatives that are differentiated from it.

In the first place, the biblical witness to creation participates in the matrix of religious experience in general, which it specifies in a definite way. The following considerations are part of this foundational matrix of religious experience: (1) Religious experience refers at the same time to the whole of reality and to personal destiny; (2) it presupposes and makes a fundamental (metaphysical) distinction, namely, between fleeting and defective reality as it is in fact and the authentic, true, redeemed, and perfected reality, a portion of which can be obtained under certain conditions even in the midst of this present world; and (3) both the ability to distinguish between the two worlds and also the redeeming and perfecting passage out of the old and into the new "world" are an event, that is, are experienced as a gift, which thereby becomes at the same time a duty to act responsibly.

During the crucial period in the development of religion and culture (between 800 and 200 B.C.), the still relatively undifferentiated archaic religiosity was replaced by differentiated types of increasingly more distinct and universal cosmocentric, historiocentric, and psychocentric religions, which had alternative ways of approaching the problem of mediating between the two worlds that had come apart: chiefly by way of the cosmos in the cosmocentric religions, chiefly by way of spirit and interiority in the psychocentric religions, and chiefly by way of history in the historiocentric religions. If cosmos, history, and spirit are fundamental aspects of human existence, then these three media and loci of religious experience cannot be entirely absent from any type of religion.

In all three basic types of religious experience, the world comes into view, first and foremost the immediate world in which one lives, but then also the world as a whole (insofar as the fundamental religious distinction is made explicit), but the latter occurs in a wide variety of ways.

The uniqueness of Israel's faith in Yahweh, in the structural history of religion, consists in the fact that here two fundamental religious experiences, namely, the transcendence of the Most-High Creator God and the nearness of the historical God of salvation and family, are fused together. Then, from the Exilic period on, Israel's expressly monotheistic profession of faith in God also affirmed that Yahweh, the historical covenant God of Israel, is the Creator of the world, and the Creator of the world is the God of Israel. As the multiplicity of creation myths shows, the world and its religious origin are the object of a distinct religious experience. Israel, too, participates in it. On the other hand, this belief in creation becomes really relevant and conscious in Israel only in the sixth century before Christ, during the Exilic period, and this occurs in connection with a radical crisis of faith in the Yahweh of salvation history. Here, on the one hand, this faith serves as the foundation of salvation history, and, on the other hand, creation itself becomes part of history in that faith. It appears now as the beginning of a salvation history and furthermore, in the midst of historical crises, as a new creation, indeed, finally as the definitive new creation at the end of time.

As a consequence of the differentiation of faith and reasoning in antiquity, various forms of reflection on the belief in creation arose. The magisterial declarations connected with such disputes are intended primarily to make negative statements, that is, they are essentially aimed against erroneous interpretations of the belief in creation, in the first place, against monism (the Neoplatonic doctrine of emanation, the Aristotelian notion of the eternity of the world, and pantheism) and, secondly, against Gnostic dualism (Gnosticism, Manichaeism, and so on). In this negative intention, they are relevant to all subsequent dogmatic reflection.

2.3 Belief in Creation in Keeping with Reason

Practically speaking, in order to complete this third dogmatic step of demonstrating the intelligibility and reasonability of belief in creation, many very different approaches from metaphysics, the philosophy of science, and epistemology are used.

As already noted, in order to distinguish between belief in creation and the theory of evolution and to define their intersection, I use a transcendental-philosophical approach, one that Richard Schaeffler has developed in a combination of transcendental, historico-empirical, and semiotic reflection.

2.3.1 Distinguishing creation and nature, the doctrine of creation and the theory of evolution, religious faith, and science

Scholars on the theological side are still in agreement that these pairs of concepts should be distinguished, but they no longer agree about what the difference consists of. However one may conceptualize the difference between belief in creation and evolutionary theory (often, for example, as the That and the How of the cosmogony[4]),[5] typically a distinction is used, the distinction between *creatio originalis* (the original creation) or *creatio ex nihilo* [creation out of nothing] and *creatio continua* (the preservation of the world), which is followed then in traditional theology also by *providentia* (providence) and the *concursus divinus* (God's cooperation with creatures). The real difference is then usually

[4] Eberhard Schockenhoff, "Kann man glauben, um zu erkennen? Evolutionslehre und 'Intelligent Design', gesehen im Licht einer Theologie der Schöpfung", *Frankfurter Allgemeine Zeitung*, no. 199 (August 27, 2005): 44.

[5] See the summaries in Ulrich Lüke, *"Al Anfang schuf Gott ..."* Bio-Theologie: Zeit–Evolution–Hominisation, 2nd ed. (Paderborn, 2001), 109–48.

seen in the *creatio ex nihilo* or *creatio originalis*, which on account of its timelessness cannot exhibit a point of intersection with the theory of evolution.

In contrast, the *creatio continua*, the preservation of the world, appears to coincide temporally with evolution; with that, a common point of intersection between belief in creation and evolutionary theory is immediately available, which is thought to require explanation.

Now it is true that these traditional theological distinctions within the concept of God's working or acting are not meaningless from the perspective of the creature, just as the distinction of various levels in the concept of creation can be quite helpful.[6] But we must be careful here that they do not jeopardize the unity of the divine work (original creation, later maintenance service and repairs, overall responsibility, guaranteeing impulses for innovation, and so on) and introduce a temporal element (two or more successive actions of God) into the concept of creation, which is inadmissible. One must therefore aim at a unified concept of creation.[7]

As noted, I make use of the transcendental theory of experience that R. Schaeffler has developed. One great advantage thereof is that it starts with a decidedly pluralistic approach: The fact that reality confronts me as a variegated world of objects, knowledge, and experience is connected with various ways of experiencing and knowing, each of which exhibits a different ordered structure and therefore constitutes a different world of objects: for instance, the world of religious objects, that of scientific objects, or of aesthetic,

[6] See especially Kessler, "Schöpfung V", 233–35, who distinguishes three levels in the concept of creation.
[7] So, too, Lüke, *"Al Anfang schuf Gott . . ."*, 150–53.

ethical, or economic objects. In this respect, it is strictly true that insofar as I experience the world scientifically, I do not experience it religiously, and vice versa. And the objects of science, too, are unlike the objects of the world of religion. In this respect, when we speak about the relation between creation and nature, the doctrine of creation and the theory of evolution, religious faith and scientific knowledge, we are dealing with clear alternatives; hence they must not be mixed together.

On the other hand, it is not a question of opposites; they just represent different forms of experience and knowledge, in which one responds in different ways to the demand of reality. Therefore, they have their own bases for objectivity, in each case the respective ordered structure of consciousness, which proves its worth again and again in the training of new generations in this specific experiential capacity and in the ongoing construction of communicative contexts for action and of worlds of experience.

This means now, applied to the concept of creation, that it should be developed first as a transcendental concept. That is to say, a religious object is not meant in the first place—a creative act of God, for instance, or its result (nature and man as God's creatures)—but rather a structural characteristic of the capacity for religious experience, the ability of religious faith to experience and to recognize the world as God's creation.

This ability is learned, practiced, and perfected through participation in the religious sign-world of a religious faith community, in the religious composition and understanding of signs. With regard to the belief in creation, it is in particular the "protological" accounts, the accounts of the beginning and origin of everything that exists, the creation stories, that structure faith consciousness and thereby enable man "to conceptualize the overall context of his everyday experience in terms of the reasons that make that context possible".[8] In this respect, they convey no new knowledge, neither empirical nor supraempirical, and hence they have no reference to an object, either. They have, rather, a transcendental and hermeneutic function. For in the light of these religious accounts and stories the believer who hears them is supposed to learn to understand the identity and totality of reality in the multiplicity of events and changes as well as in the paradox and inconsistency of their forms.

In this transcendental concept of creation, the traditional distinction between various forms of God's work has no meaning. Creation is the a priori of the world, whatever and however the latter may be. This concept of creation might also encompass the distinction between the temporal beginning of the world and an eventual "eternity" of the world. Presumably God's transcendence and freedom do not necessarily have to be tied to a temporal beginning of creation. Viewed in this way, no scientific model of the world would be excluded a priori.[9]

On the other hand, there has to be some way to mediate between this transcendental concept of creation and the world as it is understood scientifically. In the long run no human being can live in neatly separated worlds and within horizons of consciousness that are completely isolated from each

[8] Richard Schaeffler, "Aussagen über das, was 'Im Anfang' geschah: Von der Möglichkeit, sie zu verstehen und auszulegen", *Internationale katholische Zeitschrift "Communio"* 20 (1991): 4:342.

[9] See also Max Seckler, "Was heißt eigentlich 'Schöpfung'? Zugleich ein Beitrag zum Dialog zwischen Theologie und Naturwissenschaft", in *Der Kosmos als Schöpfung: Zum Stand des Gesprächs zwischen Naturwissenschaft und Theologie*, ed. Johann Dorschner, 200–202 (Regensburg, 1998).

other. The story goes that the physicist Faraday always carefully locked his laboratory behind him when he went to
his room to pray, and vice versa, but that is no long-term
solution.

2.3.2 On the intersection between God's creative work and the scientifically observed events in nature and history

Theologians today agree to a great extent that there must
be some sort of intersection between God's creative work
and the empirical reality of the world, but not about what
this intersection consists of. One very widespread mediation makes use of an ontological scheme: God works in the
world as First Cause by means of secondary causes, namely,
the forces of nature and of man. To some extent today (especially in magisterial documents) there is insistence, at least
at certain points, on a direct intervention of God in the
world. To some extent, however, a place within the scientifically discernible constitution of the world is sought in
which God's working could be localized.[10]

For all its emphasis on the pluralism of ways of knowing
and experiencing, Schaeffler's transcendental theory of experience simultaneously offers the possibility of identifying a
point of intersection among these ways of experiencing.
Because in our different attempts at an answer we continue
to refer to the unity of what is real and of its claim on us
and to the identity of our nature as acting subjects, there is
interference not only among the worlds of experience, but
also among the ways of experiencing and, thus, overlap-
ping and interactions between the individual domains. This
state of affairs means that the various ways of experiencing

[10] See Lüke, *"Al Anfang schuf Gott . . ."*, 109–48.

189

or forms of reasoning, while autonomous, are nevertheless not self-sufficient, as Schaeffler puts it. Therefore the specific limitation and endangerment of any given perspective can be overcome only by learning from one another, by a process of mutual correction and intersubjective dialogue. Due to the pluralism of ways of experiencing, the overall context that gives meaning to each individual way of experiencing also includes whatever does not correspond to that particular way of experiencing, [that is,] the totality of reality; therefore the objective truth value of experiential statements (whether they are of a scientific, religious, ethical, or aesthetic sort) is proved precisely in the dialogue between subjects who are determined by different horizons of experience or forms of reasoning.

In such successful acts of intersubjective communication and argumentation (whether as a critique of what is false, the learning of something new, or the understanding of the other), we admittedly gain no concept of the universal reasoning subject and of the unity of the world. Rather, one's own perspectival concept of subject and reason is thereby corroborated, as Schaeffler says, as a likeness and anticipation of the all-encompassing act "I think", whereas one's own perspectival world-concept is thereby corroborated as a likeness and anticipation of the unity of the real. The minimum requirement for the conduct of such a dialogue is that the foreign way of experiencing and world of experience find a place in one's own way of experiencing and world of experience.

Is there, then, in the theological understanding of God's creating and working, a place in which the scientific understanding of the world and the category of causality implied therein takes on relevance? To this end, the one concept of creation should now be developed as a more categorical concept. For here we are dealing with statements about the world of religion and with religion itself, that is, with the ideas, concepts, theories, but also with the signs and testimonies, the Sacred Scriptures, traditions, institutions, and so on. The statements "the world is a creation of God" and "God is the Creator of the world" are now part of this religious world that builds up religious consciousness by means of its ordered horizon of consciousness. Admittedly, the guiding perspectives and thought patterns are still of a religious sort (and not scientific, ethical, or aesthetic), but this religious world interferes with the other worlds and can never exist entirely alone. The religious world of ideas must be in some correlation with the everyday or scientific or ethical world of ideas, and of course vice versa. That is why the plane of intersection between belief in creation and the theory of evolution is to be found above all within the framework of the categorical concept of creation.

2.3.3 The peculiarity of the theological concept of cause and effect and its relation to causality in nature

It is very easy for all sorts of everyday or cultural notions to enter into the idea of God's action and working. Quite influential, for example, is the production model, that is, a transitive understanding of action. From the perspective of such models of action, it then seems obvious to separate God's action and his working temporally and objectively:

In the beginning God created the world out of nothing; then he has to maintain the stability of this created world (the preservation of creation) and also continue to care for his creatures, to work together with them (concurrence), but then again also bring about something surprisingly new (transition from matter to spirit, the creation of the human soul, crucial points in salvation history) and extraordinary (miracles). A theological causal principle understood in this way must then logically run the risk of becoming the competitor of worldly causes.

Before we make the categorical concept of creation concrete and divide it up mentally in this way, we should once more make an effort to understand its uniform complex structure.

If we summarize how God's action and working are related to the world of creation in religious testimonies (prayer, narratives, liturgy), how God creates, acts, and works, then the following features are decisive. (I refer here in particular to the works of R. Schaeffler.)[11]

1. The created world is completely and absolutely dependent upon the divine work.

This dependence or being-caused is, however, of a special sort. It is a dependence that makes [a subject] free and a being-caused that makes [a thing] self-contained. Creative causation and effect means being released into selfhood, empowerment for autonomy. God is the one who makes it possible for the world and man to make. Being and life are a gift that, in being received, turns into proper action.

[11] On this topic, see especially Richard Schaeffler, "Der Kultus als Weltauslegung", in *Kult in der säkularisierten Welt*, by Balthasar Fischer et al., 22–57 (Regensburg, 1974); Schaeffler, "Kultisches Handeln: Die Frage nach Proben seiner Bewährung und nach Kriterien seiner Legitimation", in *Ankunft Gottes und Handeln des Menschen: Thesen über Kult und Sakrament*, by R. Schaeffler and P. Hünermann (Freiburg, 1977), 9–50; Schaeffler, *Das Gebet und das Argument: Zwei Weisen des Sprechens von Gott: Eine Einführung in die Theorie der religiösen Sprache* (Düsseldorf, 1989), 97–162; and Schaeffler, "Aussagen über das, was 'Im Anfang' geschah".

2. God's creating and working are a personal freedom-event.

They include the free cooperation of the creature, of the world, and of man. God works in that at every moment he has already worked and now allows nature and man to work. Conversely, the effectiveness of faith-motivated action in the liturgy and in worldly service, as well as the effectiveness of natural and societal forces, is based on the fact that they constitute the form in which the divine work of establishment is made present again and again. The world's reality is based on the constant renewal of the Deity's operation. God's creative work becomes effective by means of the semiotic form of faith-based human action (in liturgy and in lived practice) as well as through world events in nature and society. Only in this creative operation of God, which is communicated through signs, are the freedom and salvation of the creature possible.

3. God's creative work has in this respect a dialectic structure.

It can be expressed with the help of spatial and temporal metaphors. If God were only far off, the creature could not be and live. If he were immovably near, the creature likewise could not be and live. His creative working is at the same time closeness and distance, the gift of a secure "environment" and the aloofness that allows room for selfhood, comparable to the dialectic of parental closeness to and distance from a child, which is a necessary condition for successful socialization and individuation. Or in a temporal version: The divine event of founding the world occurred "in the beginning" or at the origin. In order for it to be able effectively to renew the being and life of the world and of man, this event itself requires constant renewal. This renewal is effected by means of signs, especially through the liturgical recitation of the foundational accounts and through worship services, but also through service in the world and the course of world events, happenings in nature.

4. Hence the world as creation has a form that is just as sacramental as God's creating.

We are talking about a sacramental efficacy. Sacramental action is a strictly semiotic action. Without the religious, sacramental semiotic action of the faith community, God's work can have neither place nor time nor form nor efficacy within the world and the faith community. But what this semiotic action conveys—when carried out correctly—is not the will or the force of this world, but rather the nearness of God, without which the world cannot continue and life has no foundation and no purpose.

5. The world as creation also has a dialogical-temporal form.

The relation of God to the world and of the world to God has the character of a dialogue and thus of a way, which comprises action and reaction, call and answer, estrangement and conversion, guilt and forgiveness, love and love returned. Even with such a categorical concept of God's creative work, there is still a whole series of problems that, in my opinion, are not resolved satisfactorily. Although the Christian concept of creation has an irrevocably personalistic aspect and is also retained, the confrontation with religious alternatives, for instance from Indian or Chinese religions, is by no means over yet.[12] When the religious category of

---

[12] For examples of recent preliminary discussions, see Robert Cummings Neville, *Behind the Masks of God: An Essay toward Comparative Theology* (Albany, N.Y.: State University of New York Press, 1991); François Jullien, *Procès ou création: Une Introduction à la pensée chinoise: Essai de problématique interculturelle* (Paris: Seuil, 1996).

causality is understood in an essentially personal way, the relation to nature can be asserted only in an analogous sense. In order for analogous freedom to be possible in nature also, one must be able to distinguish various degrees of freedom. Of course this is completely ruled out only in strictly materialistic or dualistic approaches.

Moreover, how far the spatial allocation can or should go is still a problem. If the question of God's action and working is reduced to the question of how one should imagine God's influence on the world, how God's causality is compatible with worldly causalities, then it seems that one has to assign to God's working a specific place in the scientific understanding of the world. Today there are various suggestions, but all are problematic in one way or another. Attempts of this sort refer, for example, (1) to the non-deterministic character of microscopic and macroscopic systems, (2) to the possibility in complex systems that not only do the events on the lower levels influence the behavior of the entire system ("bottom-up causality"), but also the state of the entire system influences the events on the lower levels ("top-down causality"), (3) to the fact that in a non-dualistic understanding of body and mind, or matter and spirit, causality can be thought of as the transference of information (and not as the transference of energy).[13]

[13] Arthur Robert Peacocke, *Chaos and Complexity: Scientific Perspectives on Divine Action* (Vatican City: Vatican Observatory; Berkeley, Calif.: Center for Theology and the Natural Sciences, 1997), 138–85; J.C. Polkinghorne, *Belief in God in an Age of Science* (New Haven: Yale University Press, 1998), 48–75; Polkinghorne, *Faith, Science and Understanding* (New Haven and London: Yale University Press, 2001), 103–52; Hans-Dieter Mutschler, *Physik und Religion: Perspektiven und Grenzen eines Dialogs* (Darmstadt, 2005), 244–79.

2.3.4 The multiform character of God's work, the multiform character of the God-world relation, and the Intelligent Design debate

The latest debate over Intelligent Design, no doubt, took a very unfortunate turn. Actually the opinion piece by Cardinal Schönborn that was published in *The New York Times* on July 7, 2005, intended simply to defend the content of the Christian belief in creation and its reasonableness, along with the possibility of a natural knowledge of God, against an ideologically self-contained theory of evolution, which cites the random character of evolution and therefore declares all discourse about a divine creator and his work in the world as nonsense and irrational; to this end the essay made use of the idea of order and the idea of finality (discernible order in creation, providence).

Yet, as the subsequent discussion showed, there are in this essay expressions that seem to encroach on the autonomy of scientific research and could even be understood as a step toward American creationism.[14] Now Intelligent Design theories, insofar as they understand themselves to be scientific theories or biological science and bring the divine Creator into the picture as the explanatory basis for scientifically observable phenomena, are problematic, not only scientifically and philosophically, but also theologically.[15] For the differentiation of faith and knowledge and the

[14] Christoph Schönborn, "Finding Design in Nature", *The New York Times*, July 7, 2005: Op-Ed A 23. Immediately afterward the topic was widely discussed in the media.

[15] See Gregory R. Peterson, "The Intelligent-Design Movement", *Zygon* 37, 1 (2002): 7–23; Niall Shanks, *God, the Devil and Darwin: A Critique of Intelligent Design Theory* (Oxford: Oxford University Press, 2004); "Intelligent Design", article in Wikipedia, the free encyclopedia, 2005.

differentiation of various forms of rationality are not just something that theology is doomed to put up with, but are pursued and promoted by the Christian faith as well.[16] In a broader sense, however, this debate is concerned not just with the claim that belief in God and in creation is rational, but also and more specifically with the question of whether the creation-character of the world is knowable and detectable. From the theory in the Old Testament Wisdom literature to the present-day apologetic, this is seen especially in the orderliness and purposefulness of the world and is expressed in discourse about God's plan of creation, about the order of creation, and so on.

Such an explanation of the world belongs, no doubt, to the Christian faith tradition. To defend it and to communicate it are a basic theological and pastoral duty.

In order to do this convincingly, however, one must avoid arguments that jump to conclusions. At the very least, one must take note dogmatically of the complexity of God's working in the basic structure of the Christian faith. If we start again from the basic trinitarian structure of the Christian faith and, against this backdrop, organize the biblical and theological tradition and the groups of metaphors used therein for God's work and action in the world, the result is not only references to an order of creation, to a creative plan of God, and so on, but a much more complex answer:[17]

[16] See the summary by Siegfried Wiedenhofer, "Theologie als Wissenschaft: Eine theologische Revision", in *Bindung an die Kirche oder Autonomie? Theologie im gesellschaftlichen Diskurs*, ed. Albert Franz, 90–124 (Freiburg, 1999).

[17] On this subject, see Guy-Marie Bertrand, *La Révélation cosmique dans la pensée occidentale* (Montréal: Bellarmin, 1993); Jörg Villwock, *Die Sprache–Ein "Gespräch der Seele mit Gott": Zur Geschichte der abendländischen Gebets- und Offenbarungsrhetorik* (Frankfurt am Main, 1996); Reinhold Bernhardt, *Was heißt "Handeln Gottes"? Eine Rekonstruktion der Lehre von der Vorsehung* (Gütersloh, 1999).

God's presence in the world is the interpenetration of his cosmic presence (creation as the ordered context determined by God's wisdom from which God's voice speaks), his (salvation-) historical presence (salvation history as the expression of God's guiding, saving, liberating, forgiving, and healing action in history, with Jesus Christ as the climax), and his interior-spiritual presence (union with God in prayer, worship, and mysticism).[18]

In the actualistic or "action model", which makes use especially of metaphors drawn from creative human action, the exercise of royal dominion and the judicial administration of justice, God appears principally as a transcendent, personal acting authority. This model is problematic on account of its anthropomorphic concept of acting: such discourse concerns spontaneously caused, individual interventions, which intentionally bring about specific changes in world events according to the model of the ends-and-means relation. Hence the model as such must be expanded, for instance, through a distinction between instrumental-productive action and informative-communicative action, as well as by including the expressive and playful element in the concept of action.

In the sapiential-ordinative or "order model", which makes use of metaphors drawn from structure-forming, teleologically ordering work, for instance, the work of organic growth, the rational planning of goal-oriented series of events, or the construction of complete mechanical artifacts, the divinely configured order of being is central. This model is problematic because of its (temporal or transcendental) restriction of the divine work to the level of establishing creation,

[18] On the following discussion, see Bernhardt, *Was heißt "Handeln Gottes"?* 440–42.

as well as its tendency to deism (God as the all-wise builder of the world-machine) or pantheism (God as world-soul, the world as his body) or even determinism.

In the model of operative presence, or of internal force field, which makes use of metaphors drawn from inter- and transpersonal energies, for instance, the power of love or the consoling, protective, and sheltering presence of a significant Other, the stabilizing surrounding presence of healing environs, God's work appears as a supernatural, supramechanical and suprapersonal force, along the lines of pan-entheism [God-in-everything]. The model is problematic because its notions of God's working have impersonal connotations and also because it imagines the God-world relation to be a sort of emanation.

If we consider that these three models of God's working, or of God's presence, reflect the three fundamental religious experiences of God according to the Christian profession of faith (transcendental Creator God, historical Redeemer God, and interior Perfecter God), then the hermeneutic consistency of the creed implies that no model can be regarded in isolation. As models they have meaning only insofar as they determine, complement, and correct one another.[19] Every attempt to absolutize or isolate the idea of the order of creation is therefore theologically dangerous.

The biblical belief in creation itself, moreover, has very different experiential and motivational foundations. Among these is certainly also the experience of the orderliness and beauty of the world. The predominant point of departure for religious experience and the interpretation of the world as creation, nevertheless, is not the experience of the

[19] Bernhardt disagrees, opting for the model of operative presence as the fundamental model; ibid., 441f.

profusion, the beauty, and the well-ordered character of the world ("Trink, o Auge, was die Wimper hält, von dem goldnen Überfluss der Welt" [Drink, O eye, as much as the eyelash holds, of the golden profusion of the world], Gottfried Keller says at the conclusion of his poem "Abendlied" [Evening song]), but rather the all-encompassing fundamental experience of the ambivalence and instability of reality, the association of becoming and passing away, the constant threat to being from nothingness, to order from chaos, to life from death, and the omnipresence of suffering, negativity, evil, and calamity. Hence the belief in creation, from its very origin, has been part of religious soteriology, a counterfactual certainty that provides hope and permanence: Despite all appearances, the world has a good and reliable foundation.[20]

Theologically, therefore, the idea of the created order and the plan of creation and thus also the notion of an intelligent design must be used with great caution. Whenever the question of theodicy, soteriology, and eschatology are deliberately overlooked in this regard, the belief in creation, too, runs the risk of being misunderstood.

3

Summary

The dogmatic exposition of the Christian belief in creation has led to the following result:

[20] See Mircea Eliade, *Cosmos and History: The Myth of the Eternal Return*, trans. Willard R. Trask (New York: Harper, 1959); Siegfried Wiedenhofer, "Zur religiösen Hermeneutik des Bösen", in *Leben durch Zerstörung? Über das Leiden in der Schöpfung: Ein Gespräch der Wissenschaften*, by Hans Kessler, 181–204 (Würzburg, 2000).

With respect to the system and the way of faith (first and second steps), the concept of creation proves to be embedded in many ways in the fundamental experience of the Christian faith and in a multiplicity of very different forms of testimony over the course of history. We are dealing here with an extremely complex concept that is full of tensions. With respect to its reasonableness (third step), the uniform concept of creation should be elaborated (1) as a transcendental concept and at the same time (2) as a categorical concept.

In the first case, creation is a central part of the consciousness-structure of the Christian faith, which ensures, among other things, that the question of salvation—which is precarious, given the ambivalence of the world—obtains an answer worthy of hope, even in the worst crisis. In this respect there is no intersection with scientific knowledge of the world and hence no conflict, either.

In the second case (categorical concept of creation), creation is part of the religious world, part of the religious world of ideas. Here an intersection with the philosophical and scientific understanding of the world is unavoidable. Belief in creation makes claims to rationality and truth, and if these are to be demonstrated, some mediation between the world of faith, on the one hand, and the world of thought and knowledge, on the other, is necessary. Such mediation must in any case include the fundamental difference in their respective ways of experiencing.

Bibliography

Ahn, Gregor. "Schöpfer/Schöpfung I. Religionsgeschicht-lich". In *Theologische Realenzyklopädie*, 30:250–58. 1999.

————, Reinhard G. Kratz, Hermann Spiekermann, et al. "Schöpfer/Schöpfung". In *Theologische Realenzyklopädie*, 30:250–355. 1999.

Bayer, Oswald. "Schöpfer/Schöpfung VIII. Systematisch-theologisch". In *Theologische Realenzyklopädie*, 30:326–48. 1999.

Bernhardt, Reinhold. *Was heißt "Handeln Gottes"? Eine Rekonstruktion der Lehre von der Vorsehung.* Gütersloh, 1999.

Bertrand, Guy Marie. *La Révélation cosmique dans la pensée occidentale.* Montreal: Bellarmin, 1993.

Eliade, Mircea. *Cosmos and History:The Myth of the Eternal Return.* Translated by Willard R. Trask. New York: Harper, 1959.

Elsas, Christoph. "Schöpfung 1. Religionsgeschichtlich". In *Evangelisches Kirchenlexikon*, 3rd ed., 4:92–97. Göttingen, 1996.

Elsas, Christoph, James L. Crenshaw, Friedrich Wilhelm Horn, et al. "Schöpfung". In *Evangelisches Kirchenlexikon*, 3rd ed., 4:92–109. Göttingen, 1996.

Ganoczy, A., H.-J. Klimkeit, P. Schreiner, and R. Malek. "Welt/Schöpfung". In *Lexikon der Religionen: Phänomene—Geschichte—Ideen*, ed. Hans Waldenfels, 698–707. Freiburg, 1992.

Greshake, Gisbert. *Der dreieine Gott: Eine trinitarische Theologie.* 2nd ed. Freiburg, 1997.

Gruber, Franz. *Im Haus des Lebens: Eine Theologie der Schöpfung.* Regensburg, 2001.

Gunton, Colin E. *The Triune Creator: A Historical and Systematic Study.* Grand Rapids, Mich.: William B. Eerdmans, 1998.

"Intelligent Design". In *Wikipedia, the Free Encyclopedia.* 2005.

International Theological Commission. "Communion and Stewardship: Human Persons Created in the Image of God". July 23, 2004. http://www.vatican.va/roman_curia/

congregations/cfaith/cti_documents/rc_con_cfaith_doc_
20040723_communion-stewardship_en.html.

Jullien, François. *Procès ou création: Une introduction à la pensée chinoise: Essai de problématique interculturelle.* Paris: Seuil, 1996.

Kasper, Walter. "Dogmatik als Wissenschaft: Versuch einer Neubegründung". *Theologische Quartalschrift* 157 (1977): 189–203.

Kessler, Hans. "Gott, der kosmische Prozeß und die Freiheit: Vorentwurf einer transzendentaldialogischen Schöpfungstheologie". In *Gott, der Kosmos und die Freiheit: Biologie, Philosophie und Theologie in Gespräch,* ed. Gotthard Fuchs and Hans Kessler, 189–232. Würzburg, 1996.

―――. "Schöpfung V. Systematisch-theologisch". In *Lexikon für Theologie und Kirche,* 3rd ed., 9:230–36. Freiburg, 2000.

Kratz, Reinhard G., and Hermann Spiekermann. "Schöpfer/Schöpfung II. Altes Testament". In *Theologische Realenzyklopädie,* 30:258–83. 1999.

Kraus, Georg. *Welt und Mensch: Lehrbuch zur Schöpfungslehre.* Frankfurt am Main, 1997.

Lüke, Ulrich. *"Als Anfang schuf Gott . . ." Bio-Theologie: Zeit—Evolution—Hominisation.* 2nd ed. Paderborn, 2001.

Maier, Bernhard, Erich Zenger, Rudolf Hoppe, et al. "Schöpfung". In *Lexikon für Theologie und Kirche,* 3rd ed., 9:216–39. Freiburg, 2000.

Mohn, Jürgen. "Schöpfungsvorstellungen (Anfang und Ende)". In *Handbuch Religionswissenschaft: Religionen und ihre zentralen Themen,* ed. Johann Figl, 612–27. Innsbruck and Vienna, 2003.

Moltmann, Jürgen. *God in Creation: A New Theology and the Spirit of God.* Translated by Margaret Kohl. San Francisco: Harper and Row, 1985.

————. *The Trinity and the Kingdom: The Doctrine of God*. Translated by Margaret Kohl. New York: Harper & Row, 1981.

Mutschler, Hans-Dieter. *Physik und Religion: Perspektiven und Grenzen eines Dialogs*. Darmstadt, 2005.

Neville, Robert Cummings. *Behind the Masks of God: An Essay toward Comparative Theology*. Albany, N.Y.: State University of New York Press, 1991.

Pannenberg, Wolfhart. *Systematic Theology*. Translated by Geoffrey W. Bromiley. Grand Rapids, Mich.: Eerdmans, 1991–1998. Vol. 2.

Peacocke, Arthur Robert [A. R.]. *Theology for a Scientific Age: Being and Becoming—Natural, Divine and Human*. Oxford and Cambridge, Mass.: Blackwell, 1990.

Peterson, Gregory R. "The Intelligent-Design Movement". *Zygon* 37, 1 (2002): 7–23.

Polkinghorne, John C. *Belief in God in an Age of Science*. New Haven, Conn.: Yale University Press, 1998.

————. *Faith, Science and Understanding*. New Haven and London: Yale University Press, 2001.

Ricoeur, Paul. "Penser la Création". In *Penser la Bible*, by André LaCoque and Paul Ricoeur, 57–102. Paris: Seuil, 1998.

Schaeffler, Richard. "Aussagen über das, was 'Im Anfang' geschah: Von der Möglichkeit, sie zu verstehen und auszulegen". *Internationale katholische Zeitschrift "Communio"* 20, 4 (1991): 340–51.

————. *Erfahrung als Dialog mit der Wirklichkeit: Eine Untersuchung zur Logik der Erfahrung*. Freiburg and Munich, 1995.

————. *Das Gebet und das Argument: Zwei Weisen des Sprechens von Gott: Eine Einführung in die Theorie der religiösen Sprache*. Düsseldorf, 1989.

————. "Kultisches Handeln: Die Frage nach Proben seiner Bewährung und nach Kriterien seiner Legitimation". In

R. Schaeffler and P. Hünermann, *Ankunft Gottes und Handeln des Menschen: Thesen über Kult und Sakrament*, by R. Schaeffler and P. Hünermann, 9–50. Freiburg, 1977.

_____. "Der Kultus als Weltauslegung". In *Kult in der säkularisierten Welt*, by Balthasar Fischer, 9–62. Regensburg, 1974.

_____. *Philosophische Einübung in die Theologie*. 3 vols. Freiburg and Munich, 2004.

_____. *Religion und kritisches Bewußtsein*. Freiburg and Munich, 1973.

Schockenhoff, Eberhard. "Kann man glauben, um zu erkennen? Evolutionslehre und 'Intelligent Design', gesehen im Licht einer Theologie der Schöpfung". *Frankfurter Allgemeine Zeitung*, no. 199 (August 27, 2005): 44.

Schönborn, Christoph. "Finding Design in Nature". *The New York Times*, July 7, 2005: Op-Ed A 23.

Seckler, Max. "Was heißt eigentlich 'Schöpfung'? Zugleich ein Beitrag zum Dialog zwischen Theologie und Naturwissenschaft". In *Der Kosmos als Schöpfung: Zum Stand des Gesprächs zwischen Naturwissenschaft und Theologie*, ed. Johann Dorschner, 174–214. Regensburg, 1998.

Shanks, Niall. *God, the Devil and Darwin: A Critique of Intelligent Design Theory*. Oxford: Oxford University Press, 2004.

Villwock, Jörg. *Die Sprache—Ein "Gespräch der Seele mit Gott": Zur Geschichte der abendländischen Gebets- und Offenbarungsrhetorik*. Frankfurt am Main, 1996.

Wiedenhofer, Siegfried. "Hermeneutik III. Systematisch-theologisch". In *Lexikon für Theologie und Kirche*, 3rd ed., 5:6–7. 1996.

_____. "Theologie als Wissenschaft: Eine theologische Revision". In Albert Franz, ed., *Bindung an die Kirche oder Autonomie? Theologie im gesellschaftlichen Diskurs*, ed. Albert Franz, 90–124. Freiburg, 1999.

_____. "Zur religiösen Hermeneutik des Bösen". In *Leben durch Zerstörung? Über das Leiden in der Schöpfung: Ein Gespräch der Wissenschaften*, by Hans Kessler, 181–204. Würzburg, 2000.

BIOGRAPHICAL AND
BIBLIOGRAPHICAL NOTES

Joseph Ratzinger—Pope Benedict XVI
"Schöpfungsglaube und Evolutionstheorie". In *Wer ist das eigentlich—Gott?* ed. H.J. Schulz, 232–45. Munich, 1969. Also in *Dogma und Verkündigung*. 4th ed. 143–56. Donauwörth, 2005.

In the Beginning: A Catholic Understanding of the Story of Creation and the Fall. Translated by Boniface Ramsey. Grand Rapids, Mich.: Eerdmans, 1995 [original German edition: *Im Anfang schuf Gott: Vier Münchener Fastenpredigten über Schöpfung und Fall* (Munich, 1986)].

"Geleitwort" (Preface). In *Evolutionismus und Christentum*, ed. R. Spaemann, P. Koslowski, and R. Löw, vii–ix. Weinheim, 1986.

"The Truth of Christianity?" In *Truth and Tolerance: Christian Belief and World Religions*, 138–209. Translated by Henry Taylor. San Francisco: Ignatius Press, 2004.

Prof. Peter Schuster, Ph.D., born 1941, professor of theoretical chemistry at the University of Vienna, president of the Austrian Academy of Sciences
"From Belief to Facts in Evolutionary Theory". In *Knowledge and Belief: Wissen und Glauben*, ed. W. Löffler and

The bibliographical notes, to a great extent, were available to members of the *Schülerkreis* in advance of the meeting/conference/session.

P. Weingartner, 353–63. Wittgenstein Akten, vol. 32. Vienna: öbvahpt, 2004.

"Evolution and Design: The Darwinian View of Evolution Is a Scientific Fact and Not an Ideology". *Complexity* 11, 1 (2006): 12–15.

"'Genetic Load' und andere Gründe, warum das Leben nicht optimal sein kann". In *Das Problem des Übels in der Welt*, ed. P. Weingartner, 51–67. Frankfurt: Peter Lang, 2005.

"Was ist Leben?" In *Virtualität und Realität: Bild und Wirklichkeit in den Naturwissenschaften, Wissenschaft—Bildung—Politik*, ed. G. Magerl and K. L. Komarek, 2:114–42. Vienna: Böhlau/Österreichische Forschungsgemeinschaft, 1998; the author's contribution to the discussion is printed on pages 265–69.

"Molekulare Evolution". In *Geschichte der österreichischen Humanwissenschaften*, ed. K. Acham, vol. 2: *Lebensraum und Organismus des Menschen*, 295–328. Vienna: Passagen Verlag, 2001.

Darwin und Chemie? Die chemischen Grundlagen der biologischen Evolution. Wiener Vorlesungen im Rathaus, vol. 126. Vienna: Picus Verlag, 2006.

Prof. Robert Spaemann, Ph.D., born 1927, professor emeritus of philosophy at the Ludwig Maximilian-University in Munich

Die Frage Wozu? Geschichte und Wiederentdeckung des teleologischen Denkens. Munich-Zürich, 1981.

"Sein und Gewordensein: Was erklärt die Evolutionstheorie?" In *Evolutionstheorie und menschliches Selbstverständnis*, ed. R. Spaemann and P. Koslowski, 73–91. Weinheim, 1984.

"Einführung" (introduction). In *Evolutionismus und Christentum*, ed. R. Spaemann, R. Löw, and P. Koslowski, 1–5. Weinheim, 1986.

Prof. Paul Erbrich, S.J., Ph.D., born 1928, professor emeritus of natural philosophy at the *Hochschule für Philosophie* in Munich

Zufall: Eine naturwissenschaftlich-philosophische Untersuchung. Stuttgart, 1988.

Makrokosmos—Mikrokosmos: Ursprung, Entwicklung und Probleme der Physik. Stuttgart, 1996.

"Wie weit trägt Darwins Mechanismus von Zufall und Selektion?" In *Evolution als Schöpfung? Ein Streitgespräch zwischen Philosophen, Theologen und Naturwissenschaftlern,* ed. Paul Weingartner. Stuttgart, 2001.

Christoph Cardinal Schönborn, born 1945, Archbishop of Vienna, member of the International Theological Commission

"Schöpfungskatechese und Evolutionstheorie: Vom Burgfrieden zum konstruktiven Konflikt". In *Evolutionismus und Christentum,* ed. R. Spaemann, R. Löw, and P. Koslowski, 91–116. Weinheim, 1986.

Chance or Purpose? Creation, Evolution, and a Rational Faith. Edited by Hubert Philip Weber. Translated by Henry Taylor. San Francisco: Ignatius Press, 2007. [original German edition: *Ziel oder Zufall? Schöpfung und Evolution aus der Sicht eines vernünftigen Glaubens.* (Freiburg, 2007)].

Prof. Siegfried Wiedenhofer, Ph.D., born 1941, professor of fundamental and dogmatic theology at the *Johann-Wolfgang-Goethe-Universität* in Frankfurt

The **Schulerkreis** *of Pope Benedict XVI* developed out of colloquia for the doctoral candidates of Professor Joseph Ratzinger at the Universities of Bonn, Münster, Tübingen, and Regensburg. This circle of graduate and postgraduate students who were working on their doctoral and inaugural dissertations met for the first time for a collective theological exchange with their teacher in early 1978 after his consecration as Archbishop of Munich and his elevation to the rank of cardinal. Soon afterward, the meeting of the *Schülerkreis* with their teacher took place every summer. During these gatherings, they discussed theological and philosophical topics of current interest, some of which also involved ecumenical or interreligious issues. Usually guest speakers were invited, but occasionally members of the circle presented papers also. The theological discussions took place within a spiritual framework and were often supplemented by an exchange of experience with Cardinal Ratzinger/Pope Benedict and among the former students. With this book, the *Schülerkreis* documents for the first time the papers and discussions of such a session.

Publications: *Weisheit Gottes—Weisheit der Welt: Festschrift für Joseph Kardinal Ratzinger zum 60. Geburtstag.* Edited by W. Baier, Stephan Otto Horn, Vinzenz Pfnür, Christoph Schönborn, and Siegfried Wiedenhofer. 2 vols. Sankt Ottilien, 1987.

Joseph Cardinal Ratzinger. *Vom Wiederauffinden der Mitte: Grundorientierungen: Texte aus vier Jahrzehnten.* Edited by S. O. Horn, V. Pfnür, V. Twomey, S. Wiedenhofer, and J. Zöhrer. Published by the *Schülerkreis*, Freiburg im Breisgau, 1997.

Joseph Cardinal Ratzinger. *Pilgrim Fellowship of Faith: The Church as Communion.* Edited by S. O. Horn and V. Pfnür. Translated by Henry Taylor. San Francisco: Ignatius Press, 2005.

D. Vincent Twomey, S.V.D. *Pope Benedict XVI: The Conscience of Our Age: A Theological Portrait.* San Francisco: Ignatius Press, 2007.

Hansjürgen Verweyen. *Joseph Ratzinger—Benedikt XVI.: Die Entwicklung seines Denkens.* Darmstadt, 2007.